# Archetypal Psychotherapy

"Drawing upon numerous strands from the work of James Hillman and other authors in the field of archetypal psychology, Jason Butler weaves together a consistent approach to an archetypal psychotherapy. His book is an important contribution that situates Hillman's many contributions to archetypal theory within a context of archetypal practice. A must-read for all those who value the work of recovering soul in psychology."
—**Professor Robert D. Romanyshyn**, Pacifica Graduate Institute, USA

Archetypal psychology is a post-Jungian mode of theory and practice initiated primarily through the prolific work of James Hillman. Hillman's writing carries a far-reaching collection of evocative ideas with a wealth of vital implications for the field of clinical psychology. With the focus on replacing the dominant fantasy of a scientific psychology with psychology as logos of soul, archetypal psychology has shifted the focus of therapy away from cure of the symptom toward vivification and expression of the mythopoetic imagination.

This book provides the reader with an overview of the primary themes taken up by archetypal psychology, as differentiated from both classical Jungian analysis and Freudian derivatives of psychoanalysis. Throughout the text, Jason Butler gathers the disparate pieces of archetypal method and weaves them together with examples of dreams, fantasy images, and clinical vignettes in order to depict the particular style taken up by archetypal psychotherapy—a therapeutic approach that fosters an expansion of psychological practice beyond mere ego-adaptation and coping, providing a royal road to a life and livelihood of archetypal significance.

*Archetypal Psychotherapy: The clinical legacy of James Hillman* will be of interest to researchers and academics in the fields of Jungian and archetypal psychology looking for a new perspective, as well as practicing psychotherapists.

**Jason A. Butler** is a psychotherapist in private practice in San Francisco, USA, and a core faculty member at John F. Kennedy University, USA.

## Research in Analytical Psychology and Jungian Studies Series

Series Advisor: Andrew Samuels

*Professor of Analytical Psychology, Essex University, UK*

The *Research in Analytical Psychology and Jungian Studies* series features scholarly works that are, broadly speaking, of an empirical nature. The series comprises research-focused volumes involving qualitative and quantitative research, historical/archival research, theoretical developments, heuristic research, grounded theory, narrative approaches, collaborative research, practitioner-led research, and self-study. The series also includes focused works by clinical practitioners, and provides new research informed explorations of the work of C. G. Jung that will appeal to researchers, academics, and scholars alike.

Books in this series:

**Time and Timelessness**
Temporality in the theory of Carl Jung
*Angeliki Yiassemides*

**Apophatic Elements in the Theory and Practice of Psychoanalysis**
Pseudo-Dionysius and C.G. Jung
*David Henderson*

**C.G. Jung and Hans Urs von Balthasar**
God and evil – A critical comparison
*Les Oglesby*

**Bridges to Consciousness**
Complexes and complexity
*Nancy M. Krieger*

**The Alchemical Mercurius**
Esoteric symbol of Jung's life and works
*Mathew Mather*

**Archetypal Psychotherapy**
The clinical legacy of James Hillman
*Jason A. Butler*

# Archetypal Psychotherapy

## The clinical legacy of James Hillman

Jason A. Butler

Routledge
Taylor & Francis Group
LONDON AND NEW YORK

First published 2014
by Routledge
27 Church Road, Hove, East Sussex, BN3 2FA

and by Routledge
711 Third Avenue, New York, NY 10017

*Routledge is an imprint of the Taylor & Francis Group, an informa business*



*British Library Cataloguing in Publication Data*
A catalogue record for this book is available from the British Library

*Library of Congress Cataloging in Publication Data*
Butler, Jason A.
Archetypal psychotherapy : the clinical legacy of James Hillman / Jason A. Butler.
pages cm.—(Research in analytical psychology and Jungian studies)
1. Archetype (Psychology) 2. Psychoanalysis. 3. Hillman, James.
I. Title.
BF175.5.A72B88 2014
150.19'54092—dc23

2013042443

ISBN: 978-0-415-72545-3 (hbk)
ISBN: 978-1-315-85680-3 (ebk)

Typeset in Sabon
by RefineCatch Limited, Bungay, Suffolk

To my three fathers:
Gary—father of blood
Bruce—father of flesh
James—father of thought

# Contents

# Acknowledgments

This book would be paltry in comparison were it not for the many conversations with my dear friends. Dr. Evan Miller was integral in lighting the fire, adding the fuel, and provoking the flame, always pushing me further toward "the two-horned topics." Bryce Way taught me what it means to feel an idea and to take the risk of living that feeling.

Vida Violeta, for all the long meandering walks through graveyards, forests, and gardens, for the love you showed my dreams, and for your faery spirit, thank you. To my brother and sister, Shanna Butler and Chase Desso, your support has taught me what it means to *be* family, a gift of unimaginable value.

I owe a special debt of gratitude to two very important mentors, Dr. Robert Romanyshyn and Dr. Michael Sipiora. You gave me the gift of initiation into tradition, introducing me to a cast of characters and ideas that have been both generous and provocative. Lastly, I would like to thank Dr. Safron Rossi and OPUS archives for the great effort taken to preserve and elaborate the work of James Hillman. The time spent combing through the archival material was an adventure abundant with riches.

Chapter 1

# Introduction

One of the primary pursuits of archetypal psychology has been to "unpack the backpack" of psychology—relying heavily on a methodological stance of *via negativa*, or description through negation, and deconstruction. This position has resulted in a wealth of critique that, while often controversial and even heretical, has had a significant impact on the field of psychology. It is important to note, however, that this deconstructive approach is also one fantasy among many. A move towards seeing through this methodology invokes an immediate encounter with the dismembering influence of Dionysus, a god closely associated with revitalization through disorder. It is the Dionysian presence that facilitates the radical re-visioning and tearing apart of stale, violently fixated, and dogmatic theory and practice. Through the work of archetypal psychology, Dionysus has presented as a dialectic partner to the abhorrent one-sidedness of Apollonian natural science psychology. As necessary as this deconstruction has been, James Hillman (2005) himself has noted, every archetypal image has its own excess and intensity. Without an explicitly constructive element, the clinical implications of archetypal psychology remain largely dormant.

The various theorists contributing to the field of archetypal psychology have yet to produce a work that effectively encapsulates an archetypal approach to psychotherapy (Hillman, 2004). True to its Dionysian form, dismembered pieces of therapeutic method are strewn throughout the literature (Berry, 1982, 1984, 2008; Guggenbühl-Craig, 1971; Hartman, 1980; Hillman, 1972, 1975a, 1977a, 1978, 1979a, 1979b, 1980; Newman, 1980; Schenk, 2001; Watkins, 1981, 1984). This study is an attempt to gather the disparate pieces of archetypal method and weave them together with dreams, fantasy images, and clinical vignettes in an effort to depict the particular style taken up by archetypal psychotherapy.

While respecting the importance of deconstruction and *via negativa*, the aim of this text is to re-construct and clearly describe archetypal psychology's unique contribution to therapeutic practice. Through the careful gathering of the disparate notes on psychotherapeutic method and the mobilization of a running active imagination with Hillman's writing, or more precisely Hillman as image, this study will not only delineate an archetypal approach to psychotherapy but also amplify existing approaches to achieve a more lucid understanding of the therapeutic relevance of archetypal psychology. Throughout the text, I give very little attention to Hillman's vehement and, as David Tacey (1998) noted, projection-filled straw man arguments against psychotherapy. Instead my attention is focused on the therapeutic import embedded in Hillman's work, particularly his work with image.

Although my engagement with Hillman's work has been central to this study, it is essential to recognize the polymorphous styles of archetypal psychotherapy which have been developed by Lopez-Pedraza (1977), Berry (1982, 1984), Watkins (1981, 1984, 1986), Hartman (1980), Newman (1980), Schenk (1989), Coppin (1996), Bleakley (1995), and Giegerich, (1998), among others.

Archetypal psychotherapy will be generally defined as a depth psychological theory and praxis that aims at: "a) precise portrayal of the image; b) sticking to the image while hearing it metaphorically; c) discovering the necessity within the image; d) experiencing the unfathomable analogical richness of the image" (Hillman, 1977a, p. 82). Following C. G. Jung's (1929/1968) understanding of image as psyche, Hillman (2004) has defined this key feature of archetypal psychology as "the psyche itself in its imaginative visibility; as primary *datum*, image is irreducible" (p. 18). Edward Casey (1974) further qualified the notion of image in his well-received declaration that an image is not defined by a particular type of content, that is, a pictorial form, but by the way in which one sees, that is, an imaginal perspective. The central emphasis afforded to image within archetypal psychology qualifies the tradition as an imaginal psychology, meaning "a study of psyche . . . develop[ed] from the nature and reality of its experience, which is understood here to be images" (Watkins, 1984, p. 102).

## Introduction to archetypal psychology

James Hillman (April 12, 1926 – October 27, 2011), the initiating force and sustaining voice of archetypal psychology, was a prolific and talented writer and arguably the most influential Jungian theorist since Jung. His ideas are provocative and have, since the early days of his career, constellated strongly polarized reactions in the psychological community. Whereas his work, spanning over 50 years, covers a diverse array of topics and contains a multitude of different, even contradictory (see Tacey, 1998), moves, Hillman's opus never strays from his primary focus: the vivification and elucidation of a psychology rooted in the archetypal imagination.

After completing his degree in English Literature at the Sorbonne in Paris and a second degree in Mental and Moral Science at Trinity College in Dublin, Hillman made his way to Zurich where he trained at the Jung Institute, founded just five years prior. In March of 1953, Hillman began his training analysis with Carl Alfred Meier, one of the most central figures in the early days of the institute and an analysand of Carl Jung. While training at the Jung Institute, it did not take long for Hillman's provocative nature to make itself known.

Hillman quickly began his confrontation with orthodox Jungian ideas, some of which he would spend his career developing and some that he would vehemently reject. As the first appointed Director of Studies at the Zurich Jung Institute, intent on initiating a "process of regeneration and renewal" (as cited in Russell, 2013, p. 455), Hillman also began confronting the older generation of analysts and their well-established ideas surrounding the institute's direction. Hillman was gripped by the spirit of the new, caught in a tension-filled dialectic between the old and the young, *senex* and *puer*—an archetypal pairing that he spent significant portions of his career investigating and living.

While completing the clinical portion of his analytic training, Hillman met regularly with a group of students and a seasoned supervisor to present and critique case material. As he described in his biography, he had a distaste for the whole process, noting his observation that "everybody's talking about somebody who isn't here, it's all fantasy" (Russell, 2013, p. 421). He decided to trust his instinct, asking one of his patients as well as the supervisor leading the group if the patient could sit in on the meeting and speak for himself about his own psychological process. Although the patient agreed, the supervisor denied Hillman's request, describing his idea as "too radical" (p. 421), a condemnation that would be used often in response to Hillman's work.

True to the astrological sign of Aries under which he was born, Hillman had a martial nature, trusting his anger as his "favorite demon" (Hillman, 1991, p. 147). Hillman's work was spurred on "when something felt insulted" (Russell, 2013, p. 429). These areas of insult, which in the early days of his career revolved most notably around the prevailing interpretations of puer phenomena, were seeds for Hillman's long career of differentiating his thought from those of the classical Jungian school. Unlike many students in Zurich who fell into an unquestioning relationship with Jungian theory, Hillman retained a sense of critical thought that allowed him to take a different angle. Hillman resisted becoming an enamored devotee of Jung, calling Jung's influence a syndrome, "a kind of magical projection" (p. 426). Hillman noted: "I was so *into* the Jungian world, but at the same time something in me was protecting itself from him" (p. 426).

He held close to what he knew of the value of puer phenomena, protecting his own lived experience of this archetypal dominant from the reductive interpretations he was encountering at the Institute. At that time Marie-Louise Von Franz was offering a number of lectures on the pathology of the puer. Following Jung, she emphasized the relation between the puer and the mother and placed heavy emphasis on descent, an earthly cure for the puer, occasionally even sending her young male patients off to farms where they could get dirt in their shoes, a grounding of the youthful spirit. Hillman read this move as dreadfully literal and worked instead to deliteralize earth, "to see through, to turn into psyche, rather than have the psyche turned into earth" (as cited in Russell, 2013, p. 429).

By the early 1960s, Hillman had become close friends with Adolf Guggenbühl-Craig who, like Hillman, had a fondness for paradox and turning cherished ideas upside down. One of his more notable contributions in this regard came out of a paper he delivered while on a lecture tour through the United States with Hillman. The paper, titled "Youth and Individuality," challenged the classical Jungian notion that the individuation process begins only after one has reached mid-life, arguing that adolescence ushers in many important features of psychological individuation (Russell, 2013). Looking back on this important period, Hillman commented, "The idea was, we were trying to take down the older generation" (p. 495).

Despite the many moves Hillman made to differentiate his thought from the old guard, or "second generation Jungians" (Goldenberg, 1975), he held close to the notion of fidelity to tradition. He describes his position clearly in a 1965 letter:

> I belong to lots of things: my family tree, the places where I was taught, the school of psychology I am a member of, the country in which I have been landed in. Doctrine is part of my backbone.

> I work within one, working daily to get out, to fight it, to change it, to break it. But from within.
>
> (as cited in Russell, 2013)

It was while in the heat of this struggle with Jungian orthodoxy that Hillman began his formal exploration of the puer-senex tension per invitation to the 1967 Eranos conference. Responding to his felt sense that Jungian psychology was dominated by the negative senex and the "cult of the old" (Russell, 2013, p. 590), Hillman set out to redeem the puer from his traditional association with the mother, emphasizing instead his archetypal role in relativizing the negative senex—the oppressive force of the old wise man. Moreover, Hillman would come to demonstrate the way in which the senex and puer are requisites of each other, abiding as two ends of a polarity that is paradoxically a "union of sames" (Hillman, 2005, p. 58). His efforts to foster the "moist spark" (Hillman, 2005, p. 54) of the puer, to counter the old guard within his psychological tradition, would soon lead him to announce a distinct differentiation from orthodox Jungian psychology, initiating a new movement which he called archetypal psychology.

Hillman's first use of the title archetypal psychology arrived in an essay titled "Why Archetypal Psychology?" first published in 1970. Here he outlined a number of reasons for adopting a title other than "Jungian," "analytical," or "complex psychology." Hillman noted the need to differentiate from Carl Jung the man, leaving possession of the name to the Jung family. He also emphasized the way in which the adjective 'archetypal' "gives the psyche a chance to move out of the consulting room" and "gives an archetypal perspective to the consulting room itself" (Hillman, 1975b, p. 142). Whereas analytical and complex psychology constellate associations to a psychology of the individual, archetypal psychology broadens the scope to encompass the breadth of culture, history, and the "plurality of archetypal forms" (p. 143), a polytheistic psychology. Throughout his career, Hillman used the distinction of archetypal psychology to revision, question, critique, and discard many primary features in both Jung's psychology and psychoanalysis in general.

Hillman's position in relation to both Jung and Sigmund Freud has been to take their work and turn it in such a way as to make it his own. He stepped back from the literal work as noun and psychologized or saw through to the underlying verb, as he noted "the way in which the soil is plowed" (1999). In doing so, he has taken up what he has understood to be Jung's way of working, rather than a literal adherence to the work. Specifically, it is Jung's love of the unusual and idiosyncratic and his talent for bringing these phenomena into relation with their underlying root that makes Jung radical,[1] and in following this spirit, "Jung's daemonic inheritance," Hillman (1999) has designated himself a "true blue Jungian."

In seeing through Hillman's work, it is clear that his theories spring from a similar adherence to the unusual and idiosyncratic. Hillman has taken Jung's notion of individuation as differentiation and expanded it into a mode of theorizing as well as a mode of practicing psychology. This agenda of difference is strewn throughout the work of archetypal psychology. Importantly, this move is also essential to the practice of archetypal psychotherapy, where the work is to proceed into and enhance the difference, the unusual, to follow the idiosyncratic event into its archetypal root. As Hillman (1971) has noted, "for what else is individuation but a particularization of the soul" (p. 133).

To describe how an archetypal psychotherapy differs from a Jungian psychotherapy is an endeavor bound to be fraught with over-generalizations. Psychotherapeutic process is highly contingent on the idiosyncrasies of both the therapist and the patient, making general statements about what constitutes "Jungian" or "archetypal" therapy inherently limited. However, clear differences can be described based on the distinct theoretical emphases of these two highly related traditions.

## Differentiating Jungian and archetypal psychology

Hillman has been justifiably criticized, most notably by Tacey (1998), for his extremism in his attempt to differentiate himself from Jung, discounting the master while implicitly exaggerating the originality of his own work. One primary example can be found in Hillman's (1992) later work emphasizing the Neoplatonic notion of *anima mundi*. It takes no stretch of the imagination to notice the parallels between Hillman's anima mundi and Jung's description of the *unus mundus* (1970) and the psychoid archetype (1947/1970). Moreover, as Tacey (1998) noted, "forty years before Hillman, with much less fanfare and bravado, Jung had already (re)discovered the Neoplatonic idea of anima mundi" (p. 225).

Both Jung and Hillman were attempting to reconcile the profound rupture between spirit and matter—to spiritualize matter and to materialize spirit, arguing that soul is the intermediary space within which this connection takes place. Yet, despite the commonality of their pursuit, Hillman falsely positions Jung as only interested in psyche as inside, "whereas" Hillman stated in an unpublished lecture "for our post-jungian archetypal school, psyche is more out there, in the world" (as cited in Tacey, 1998, p. 225).

Tacey, however, has demonstrated a similar indulgence in exaggerated rhetoric, charging Hillman with a dangerously "incomplete understanding of Jung," "as if Hillman reads Jung with one eye open, and another eye shut" (Tacey, 2001, p. 116). Although Tacey highlighted several important critiques of Hillman's work, including the "conservative and simplistic appropriation of Jungian theory" (Tacey, 1997, p. ix) in the men's movement of Bly, Hillman, and Meade, a small footnote in Hillman's oeuvre, Tacey's (2001) generalization to Hillman's entire "life and work" (p. 116) stretches the critique far beyond reason.

For example, Tacey fails to account for the way in which Hillman's work with image makes profound advancements to Jung's notion of psyche as image. Hillman follows out the implications of this statement far more faithfully than Jung, who waivers from a phenomenological orientation to metaphysical essentialism. Following the metaphysical aspect of Jung's work, classical Jungian practitioners, as represented by von Franz (1996), Edinger (1992), and Neumann (1954/1995), tend to abandon the unique psychic phenomena in favor of abstraction through amplification. Alternatively, an archetypal approach aims to hold the tension between the phenomena and its essential or archetypal nature far more delicately. The unique phenomenon is given far more clinical emphasis and authority than theoretical and mythic categories.

The adherence to qualitative difference and particularity has spurred the following important critical moves that distinguish the archetypal approach from classical Jungian theory and practice: from archetype to archetypal, from symbol to image, from unconscious to imagination, from compensation to complexity of conjunctions, and from the one to the many. It is with these twists that Hillman has distanced himself from traditional Jungian psychology and formed a distinct approach called archetypal psychology. As such, it is essential to give attention to each of these differences individually.

## *Archetype to archetypal*

The psychological notion of archetype is arguably the most important contribution Jung offered to both psychology and culture. In

Jung's (1964) work, archetype has been variously defined as primordial types, universal images, "a tendency to form such representations of a motif," and "an instinctive *trend*" (p. 58). Following Kant, Jung (1950/1969) has noted that the archetype itself is unknowable; only the archetypal image falls within human experience. In response to this distinction, Hillman (2004) has discarded the study of archetype as *noumenon*, or thing-in-itself, and has instead focused his attention solely on phenomenal experience. He argued: "Archetypal psychology, in distinction to Jungian, considers the archetypal to be always phenomenal, thus avoiding the Kantian idealism implied in Jung" (Hillman, 2004, p. 14). As Roberts Avens (1980) noted, "Instead of asking how archetype and image are related (as two distinct events), one begins with 'archetypal image'" (p. 43).

This move can be described as a shift from archetypes as transcendent structures to archetypes as immanent persons—a move from the metaphysical and abstract to the imaginal and concrete, from archetype as noun to archetypal as adjective. In so doing, archetypal psychologists have attempted to discard the unnecessary metaphysics strewn throughout Jungian psychology and focus instead on furthering the rich exposition of psychological phenomenology initiated by Jung.

In an effort to remain within the parameters of psychic phenomenology—the lived experience of psyche, Hillman (1993) has posed the important argument that the archetypes are *a priori* not in genesis, because that would involve metaphysical belief outside the reach of psychological experience, but *a priori* in value. The archetypal value of an image comes prior to and shapes the personal experience. By invoking the archetypal perspective, the individual places a vivid personal experience within a universal cosmology, finding his or her place in relation to the Gods. In his use of the term Gods, Hillman (1975a) has been careful to distinguish between religious reference to Gods and his psychological use. Specifically, he noted, "Theology takes Gods literally, and we do not" (p. 169). He added:

> In archetypal psychology Gods are *imagined*. They are approached through psychological methods of personifying, pathologizing, and psychologizing. They are formulated ambiguously, as metaphors for modes of experience and as numinous borderline persons. They are cosmic perspectives in which the soul participates.
>
> (p. 169)

By turning events into experiences through imagination, this aspect of the numinous embedded in everyday experiences is disclosed.

In distinction to classical Jungian psychology, archetypal psychology suggests that any image can be justified as archetypal; it is the way in which one treats the image that facilitates its qualification as archetypal. As Hillman (1977a) noted: "The image grows in worth, becomes more profound and involving, that is, it becomes more archetypal as its patterning is elaborated" (p. 75). Imagining an image as archetypal makes it more archetypal (Avens, 1980):

> Granted, then, that the archetypal character of images consists in their polysemy (many-meaningness) and polyvalence, the adjective "archetypal" must be taken to point not to the noumenality of images but to the *value* of an image endowing it with the widest, richest, and deepest possible significance.
>
> (p. 45)

In turn, when any psychic phenomena is approached as archetypal, it too begins to swell with value, exciting the imagination, conjuring other images from myth, evoking emotion, gaining complexity and poetic depth.

The following example may help to exemplify this important distinction between Jungian and archetypal theory. Many classically trained Jungian analysts are taught to distinguish between personal dreams, expressing elements of the personal unconscious, and archetypal or big dreams, expressing elements of the collective unconscious. This hierarchical privileging of one type of dream over another and the notion that one could classify a dream as a big dream independent of the dreamer's experience of the dream places the analyst in an inflated position as arbiter of archetypal significance. From the perspective of archetypal psychology, any dream can be a big dream. In fact, perhaps there are no small dreams, only small interpretations.

### Symbol to image

The notion of symbol suggests a higher order, a metaphysical archetype or noumena, outside of or beyond the presenting phenomena—one thing is standing for something else. With a symbolic representation the manifest content points to the only partially knowable latent content, like the finger pointing to the moon. As Jung (1912/1967) noted, symbols function as "a means of expression, as bridges and pointers" (p. 330).

Whereas Jung (1912/1967) expressed a desire to "hold aloof from all metaphysical assertions" (p. 231), Hillman (1975a, 1977a) has been far more emphatic about sticking to the lived experience, discarding any interest in symbolic abstraction beyond phenomena and focusing solely on that which is experienceable: psychic reality. In his adherence to psychic reality, Hillman has closely followed Jung's (1939/1954) affirmation that psyche is image. Jung (1933/1960) was adamant in his affirmation that "What appears to us as immediate reality consists of carefully processed imagery and . . . we live immediately only in a world of images" (p. 353). Hillman (1992) echoes this same sensibility in his designation of "event itself as image" (p. 34). In addition, Jung (1933/1960) noted: "Image and meaning are identical and as the first takes shape, so the latter becomes clear. Actually the pattern needs no interpretation: it portrays its own meaning" (p. 201). Hillman aligned with this image-focused, or phenomenological, aspect of Jung's work and used it against the tendency toward symbolic abstraction found in other parts of Jung's writing and even more frequently in the secondary literature of Jungian psychology.

Although Samuels (1985) pairs the practice of archetypal psychotherapy with the classical school of Jungian analysis, noting that both schools use a classical-symbolic-synthetic method in analysis, the quote he uses from Jung to describe this approach does more to show the difference between classical and archetypal method than it does to bridge the two schools. Jung wrote:

> It is absolutely necessary to supply these fantastic images that rise up so strange and threatening before the mind's eye with some kind of context so as to make them more intelligible. Experience has shown that the best way to do this is by means of comparative mythological material.
>
> (Jung, 1936/1968, p. 33)

Whereas classical Jungian practitioners emphasize the need to contextualize the image by making links to "comparative mythological material," archetypal psychotherapy has demonstrated the way in which this kind of linking often serves as an intellectualized defense against the powerfully evocative presentation of the unique image

(Hillman, 1977b). The defensive nature of amplification is apparent in Jung's comment. He noted the "strange" and "threatening" qualities of images, implying that amplification tames the image by generalizing its particularity, dulling the edge of the razor sharp specificity of the image. As Berry (1982) has cogently argued, the image comes already embedded in the context of its presentation—intelligible in its aesthetic display. Amplification is always secondary to stepping through the clearing and entering into the world disclosed by the image.

As such, image, not symbol, has been afforded a central role in archetypal psychology. Hillman (1977a) argued that phenomenologically, symbols are never experienced: "Symbols appear, only can appear, in images and as images" (p. 65). Whereas symbols are always abstractions, images are always "particularized by a specific context, mood, and scene . . . they are precisely qualified" (p. 62).

The move from symbol to image has eliminated the focus on interpreting latent content. With image, interpretation, in the sense of explicating the meaning found beyond the presenting phenomena, is not necessary because it is not assumed that there is some other material other than that which shows itself. The image, Hillman (1979b) argued, is not a symbol pointing to something else; rather, the metaphorical value of the image is inherent to the presentation of the image itself as a precise configuration of psyche. "[Images] are the psyche itself in its imaginative visibility; as primary *datum*, image is irreducible" (Hillman, 2004, p. 18).

In working with an image, one steps into its latent meaning by deepening into its presentation as such. The configuration of particulars is the disclosure of meaning. As Avens (1980) noted: "Images, in their liberated mode are themselves embodiments of meaning; that they mean what they are and are what they mean" (p. 40).

Image-focused work is, by its nature, disturbing because it ushers in the unknown. Reading an event for its symbolic content tends to trade this disturbing quality for a reified abstraction. A patient brings a dream of a large black snake and leaves the session with conceptual notions of unfettered instinct or the unconscious, waxing moon becomes regeneration or The Feminine, reflective water becomes the feeling function or maternal holding. As Hillman (1977b) stated in an unpublished document, "to treat an image as a symbol is to run from it. . . . All too often amplification becomes a counter-phobic measure against the power of the image."

### *Unconscious to imagination*

Hillman (1991) has noted that one of the most significant expansions of Jung's psychology is the way in which he has employed the term imagination instead of unconscious. Hillman's notion of the imaginal has its origin in Jung's (1937/1968) *Psychology and Alchemy* where Jung defines imagination as the goal of the alchemical work. "*Imaginatio*," Jung wrote, "is the active evocation of (inner) images *secundum naturam*, an authentic feat of thought or ideation which . . . tries to grasp the inner facts and portray them in images true to their nature. This activity is an *opus*, a work" (p. 167). Indeed, Hillman has made this the primary *opus* of archetypal psychology.

In a comment aimed at explaining his stance in relation to the use of the notion of "the unconscious," Hillman (1991) stated, "not that there isn't unconsciousness in us all the time . . . but I won't use the word as an abstract noun to cover over the cultural implications that are in [the term] imagination" (p. 32). He added:

> Besides, the word "unconscious" is loaded with subjectivity and has become a psychologism. "Imagination" connects you at once with a tradition and with aesthetic activity. With language. It refers directly to images which Jung himself says are the main content of the unconscious.
>
> (p. 32)

With the move from unconscious to imagination, Hillman has once again stood his ground for differentiation. In calling the unconscious a psychologism, he is pointing to the way in which the word has withered into a dry concept devoid of any specificity—a dead word. As the notion has become indissolubly reified, those who use the term forget that it is a perspective, using the term instead as if "the unconscious" were an actual place. In following Jung's (1937/1968) definition of imagination as the creative act of image making, Hillman has moved from a reified notion to an operative act—an act that is indelibly fundamental to psychic reality.

In addition, Hillman (1979a) has argued that references to the unconscious carry far too many important elements lumped together as an undifferentiated mass, "collecting into one clouded reservoir all fantasies of the deep, the lower, the baser, the heavier (depressed), and the darker" (p. 42). In an effort to unpack the term and reveal its myriad diverse contents, Hillman argued:

> We have buried in the same monolithic tomb called The Unconscious the red and earthy body of the primeval Adam, the collective common man and woman, and the shades, the phantoms, and ancestors. We cannot distinguish a compulsion from a call, an instinct from an image, a desirous demand from a movement of imagination.
>
> (p. 42)

Inherent to the term unconscious is a perspectival bias toward ego consciousness. The images that present in dreams, fantasies, and complexes give no indication that they are unconscious. It is only the waking ego that is unconscious. Whereas psychological methods aimed at elucidating the perspective of the ego require the fantasy of a reified thing called the unconscious, archetypal psychology, as a psychology of image, reaches back through history to bring forward the notion of imagination, where "the ego" is simply one image among many.

Hillman has worked to enrich contemporary psychological notions with historical conceptualizations of what is now called the unconscious. For example, he has, on several occasions, described the classical practice of *memoria*—a rhetorical technique used for ordering the mind where memories are imagined as persons (Hillman, 1972, 1975a, 1983). Where now there is the unconscious, we once had the people of the imagination, and *memoria* was the imaginal art of differentiating and relating to these figures. The work of Aristotle and the Neoplatonists spoke of *memoria* as the echo of the godhead reverberating in the soul of the person—image and idea as divine heritage (Hillman, 1972). Hillman noted, "As a result, [the soul's] images had to be considered as full realities, not mere fantasies, mere hallucinations, mere projections—not anything 'mere' at all" (Hillman, 1972, p. 172).

Hillman's intent in reclaiming the art of *memoria* from the vaults of history and affording it importance as a psychological practice is one part in his long-standing move towards warding off the dead words and practices of contemporary psychology, and in turn, aligning archetypal psychology within a lineage of image-centered traditions such as Neoplatonism, Gnosticism, Kabbalism, and alchemy. Locating archetypal psychology within these traditions has allowed access to a wealth of psychological ideas that are far more phenomenologically accurate and precisely differentiated than those available in contemporary psychology. Archetypal psychologists have attempted to use the reclamation of image-centered traditions to cure psychology of its reliance on reified and overly abstract concepts like the unconscious.

### *Compensation to complexity of conjunctions*

Jungian psychology is laden with notions of opposition: ego/shadow, anima/animus, unconscious/conscious, introversion/extroversion, thinking/feeling and a variety of other opposing pairs. The relationship between these dialectic poles is, according to Jung, compensatory in nature: when one aspect manifests strongly to the conscious mind, the other will present as some unconscious content. Jung (1934/1966) argued that compensation was particularly relevant to the dynamics of dreams. He wrote:

> Every process that goes too far immediately and inevitably calls forth compensations, and without these there would be neither a normal metabolism nor a normal psyche. In this sense we can take the theory of compensation as a basic law of psychic behavior. Too little on one side results in too much on the other. Similarly, the relation between conscious and unconscious is compensatory. . . . When we set out to interpret a dream, it is always helpful to ask: What conscious attitude does it compensate?
>
> (p. 153)

For Hillman (1979a), Jung's proposed law of compensation does not fit with the phenomenology of the psyche. Hillman's primary writing on dreams, *Dream and the Underworld*, posed the argument that the fantasy of compensation initiates a move away from the presenting image. The compensatory fantasy suggests that the dream image is incomplete in itself and requires an interpretation that locates the oppositional element present in the dreamer's conscious identifications. This move effectively brings the dream out of the underworld, an imaginal space Hillman has used to describe the native terrain of the dream, a mythic realm qualified by depth, metaphorical ambiguity, shade, hiddenness, and likeness.

In addition, Hillman noted, the positioning of the presenting image as compensation for a conscious attitude inevitably constellates the heroic ego's need for action to rectify the imbalance, and under the sway of this archetypal dominant Jung's (1934/1966) notion of enantiodromia, "the regulative function of opposites" (p. 72), becomes "a literal conversion and literal self-regulation" (Hillman, 1979a, p. 79). Dream interpretation becomes an allopathic procedure in which one opposite is used to cure its pairing. This treatment, Hillman argued, "practically achieves a new literal opposition, just as one-sided as the former, necessitating another dream, another visit to the doctor, and the interminable analysis of ego addiction" (p. 79).

Importantly, it is not opposition per se that Hillman opposes; rather it is the location of the opposite outside of the presenting image. He argued:

> every psychic event is an identity of at least two positions and is thus symbolic, metaphorical, and never one-sided. Only by taking it from one side does it become so; by trying to balance it, we break its hidden harmony.
>
> (1979a, p. 80)

Oppositionalism is a perspective that becomes necessary only when one stakes claim on land outside of the dreamscape. When the waking ego crosses the bridge into the underworld, the perception of the dream's one-sided opposition dissolves into a complexity of conjunctions—"a mixture or union of 'elements' or substances" (Conjunction, 2008), the *coincidentia oppositorum* of alchemy.

Hillman (1979a) has aimed to shift the notion of opposition from a dialectic of conscious/unconscious to a more absolute opposition: life/death, where death is deliteralized to mean "the self-regulation of any position by psyche, by non-literal, metaphorical perception. In this sense . . . conjunction and . . . the identity of opposites mean the simultaneous perception by the perspectives of life and death, the natural and the psychic" (p. 79).

There is no better indication of the relativized nature of the ego and its profound limitations than the lived experience of a dream or fantasy. These concentrated psychic experiences offer clear insight regarding the ego's subordinate and marginal position in relation to the retinue of other psychic characters. Imagination, as the central mode of psychic expression, is quick to demonstrate that the heroic mode of consciousness, a style of ego consciousness bound to literality, control, and pursuit of victory, is flawed and bound in a Sisyphean pattern, directing enormous effort with little awareness given to one's impotent repetitions. Whereas the ego relies on the bright light of rationality, imagination darkens the light, initiating a loss of the certainty on which the ego perspective depends (Schenk, 2011, personal communication). As ego consciousness begins to attend to the many deaths arriving ceaselessly through imaginal process, the heroic mode of being gives way to an imaginal ego characterized by a metaphoric sensibility within which death is afforded place among and within life.

Hillman (1979a) has suggested that the dream presents as a homeopathic phenomenon, "where the cure is the disease, the healing is deeper wounding, and the newborn infant is death" (p. 82). The image has everything that is needed; no symbolic abstractions or dayworld compensations are necessary. Each dream presents the full narrative: tension, *telos*, and treatment all within the sense data of the image. This notion gives rise to a methodological stance that ushers the waking ego into the underworld terrain from which the dream was born and in which it maintains its vitality and riches.

## *The one to the many*

One of the primary points of contention Hillman has taken up in relation to Jung's work is what he has interpreted to be a collapse of the polytheistic diversity of the psyche into a monotheistic doctrine. In his essay *Psychology: Monotheistic or Polytheistic*, Hillman (1971) addressed a statement made by Jung in *Aion*: "The anima/animus stage is correlated with polytheism, the self with monotheism" (as cited in Hillman, 1971, p. 193). In addition to this statement, Jung (1951/1968) has noted that the work with the anima/animus is a stage one must go through in order to get to the more important work involving the individual's relationship to wholeness. Jung wrote:

> Anyone who wants to achieve the difficult feat of realizing something not only intellectually, but also according to its feeling-value, must for better or worse come to grips with the anima/animus problem in order to open the way for a high union, a *coniunctio oppositorum*. This is the indispensable prerequisite for wholeness.
>
> (p. 31)

Here wholeness is used synonymously with the archetype Jung termed *self*. Jung's description clearly establishes a psychic hierarchy. His work in *Aion* sets out a schema or system, used often in the secondary literature of Jungian psychology, where self subsumes and encapsulates all other archetypal propensities. As a result, Jungian theory prioritizes a relationship to the self, or ego-self axis (Edinger, 1992), over relational dynamics with the multivalent figures of psyche. These figures become "problems" to be overcome on one's way toward the self as god-image and archetype of wholeness and balance. Hillman (1971) has noted that Jung's hierarchical ordering of the psyche reflects an evolutionary fantasy of linear progress which was popular in nineteenth- and early twentieth-century scholarship: just as "anima/animus is a pre-stage of the self, so is polytheism a pre-stage of monotheism" (p. 193). This is a fantasy that arises out of a dominant imperialistic culture where polytheism and animism are deemed primitive and even childish belief systems far less developed than the transcendental monotheism, that is, the Abrahamic religions. By imagining the psyche through the monotheism of self, Jungian psychology aligns itself with the culturally profuse privileging of transcendence over imminence, one over many, and spirit over soul.

Hillman (1971) has argued that the archetypal dominant present but hidden in the notion of self is the wise old man or *senex*. With self as centerpiece, Jungian psychology becomes senex psychology and thus falls into fantasies of order and abstraction. The senex as Kronos consumes the pantheon of gods, devouring his children to retain his superior power.

The executive status afforded to the self is antithetical to an archetypal psychology for several reasons. As Hillman (1971) noted, "A primacy of the self implies rather that the understanding of the complexes at the differentiated level once formulated as a polytheistic pantheon . . . is of less significance for modern man than is the self of monotheism" (p. 193). When the complexes and their respective archetypal cores are regarded as secondary to the principle of wholeness and integration, the diverse and dynamic characters of the psyche, the Gods, with their differentiated qualities, affects, blessings, and curses become less accessible to the imagination—hidden under the giant thumb of the monotheistic self. As such, the psyche is effectively reduced to ego and self, the Gods are effectively reduced to diseases, and, within the majority of psychological schools, diseases are effectively reduced to something to be rectified through behavior modification or analysis. The Gods vanish and take with them their blessings of insight, the prolificacy of images, and the opportunity for soul-making relationships.

Hillman (1971) argued: "Until we follow Jung in examining the differentiation of wholeness with the same care that he applied to the integration of wholeness our psychology does not meet the psyche's need for archetypal understanding of its problems" (p. 207). The central task of an archetypal approach to psychotherapy is to reinvigorate the relationship with the multiple figures of psyche as beings in their own right that demand to be approached "according to [their] own principle, giving each God its due over that portion of consciousness, that symptom, complex, fantasy which calls for an archetypal background" (Hillman, 1971, p. 197). This requires the therapist to have a keen understanding of the constellation of qualities held by each archetypal dominant. Such an understanding involves primarily a relative fluency in mythology—a topic that will be given extensive attention in Chapter 3.

In suspending the amorphous notion of the self, one is brought into direct relation with the inherent multiplicity of the psyche. Each archetypal propensity contains its own order, balance, excess, intensity, and shadow. And in relating to the particular qualities presented in the specificity of the image, the practitioner closely follows the movements of psyche and works to enhance the "specification of [the image's] descriptive qualities and [its] implicit metaphors" (Vannoy-Adams, 2008, p. 111).

Instead of an ego-self axis, an archetypal psychologist might imagine a multiplicity of axes, or a "'relativization' of the ego by the imagination" (Vannoy-Adams, 2008, p. 113). This move involves a polycentric perspective. The ego is shaped by a variety of different archetypal propensities, and the organization of the corresponding psychological phenomena is imagined not as a mediation by the self, according to Hillman (1997), but by the "soul's code"—a notion that draws from the platonic concept that imagines a *daemon*, or intermediary being, who is inextricably concerned with the fate of the individual and the development of one's full character.

Clinically, this move away from amorphous and reified structures of the psyche allows for an element of surprise, spontaneity, and preservation of the unique in the consulting room. However, this refusal to reify, structuralize, and systematize the anatomy of the psyche can leave practitioners with a feeling of groundlessness. Concepts and structures alleviate the anxiety inherent to the mysterious process of engaging the psyche. In place of conceptual abstraction, archetypal psychotherapy offers a methodology that facilitates finding the unique ground of each concrete particular, which image provides, thus limiting the stultifying effect brought on by theoretical formulations. Berry (2008) has described her method in the following way:

> It is best to work from the event to the idea not the other way round: (1) begin with the living event, i.e., the image; (2) focus on the image/event, sensing into it; (3) track bits of resonance that begin to form out of the event. . . . Eventually, ideas will spring up like weeds around and through them.
>
> (p. 329)

## *Soul and spirit*

The battle taken up by archetypal psychology defending the many against domination by the one is reengaged in Hillman's soul/spirit distinction. Although Jungian psychology is an expression of soul, there is a strong propensity to lose sight of soul in favor of spirit, confusing psychotherapy with spiritual discipline and allowing the spirit's agenda to dominate over the needs of soul.

Hillman (2005) described spirit as pertaining to peak experiences, transcendence, air, and mountainous height—from which everything appears unified. Spirit bears a close relationship to Apollo "the far-sighted," the god of light and rationale foresight, a god of purity, deliberation, and discipline, twin to the chaste huntress Artemis. The spirit, in its fantasy of flight, transcendence, and peak experience, is also closely connected with the dynamics of the *puer aeternus*, the eternal youth embodied in our mythologies of the highflying Icarus, Phaeton, and Peter Pan. Hillman described the puer as "narcissistic, inspired, effeminate, phallic, inquisitive, inventive, pensive, passive, fiery, and capricious" (p. 50). The puer is the all-consuming fire of spirit—fueling the *pothos*, or unappeasable longing, inherent to any spiritual discipline.

Hillman's soul/spirit distinction places soul in the deep valley below the towering mountain of spirit (Hillman, 1975a). In the valley there is multiplicity, diversity, relationship, particularity, muddiness, fog, and mist—many things are hidden, blocked from sight. There is immediacy, humidity; it's where you get messy; there dwell the nymphs, fairies, leprechauns, ancestors, and gnomes, the myriad characters of imagination—a retinue of voices and opinions (Hillman, 2005). Here you find fertility, plurality, and moisture—exemplified in the bitter moisture of tears. In the valley of soul, there is room to contain the many experiences disavowed by spirit.

Soul is phenomenology, the actuality of experience. By walking this valley, encountering events that can be digested into embodied experiences (Hillman, 1975a), falling into the murk and mud, rubbing shoulders with the multitude of characters and the challenges and blessings constellated in these relationships, one is given the opportunity to make soul. Here archetypal psychology follows John Keats' (1899/2001) declaration "Call the world if you please, 'The vale of Soul-making.' Then you will find out the use of the world" (p. 369). Soul is not some static feature but a way of seeing, a way of being in and with the world. Soul-making is a creative fashioning of one's encounters with life.

The spiritual ideal fosters and exaggerates identification with the longings of the puer-infused spirit. When the propensities of the puer are literalized, when the reflective function is absent, the dynamics of the individual dry up for lack of psychic water—the lubricating effect of the as-if, the not-too-tight-not-too-loose, like the play of a bicycle wheel, without which it would not spin (Hillman, 2005).

When soul and spirit split through the spirit's disavowal of matter, each suffers in its isolation. In the rift between spirit and matter, the soul's wounds are forced into the body as pathology while the spirit soars after its chosen ideal. However, as Hillman (2005) has argued, the classical Jungian notion of curing the puer of his lofty ideals by grounding him with literal work is a violence to the nature of this archetypal propensity—a killing of spirit. Rather, what is required is a "puer-psyche marriage" (p. 85), in which the puer begins to ground into the metaphoric work of imaginal reflection and an aesthetic appreciation of the psyche's images.

> It means that the search and questing be a psychological search and questing, a psychological adventure. It means that the messianic and revolutionary impulse connect first with the soul and be concerned first with its redemption. This alone makes human the puer's message, at the same time reddening the soul into life. It is in this realm of the soul that the gifts of the puer are first needed.
>
> (Hillman, 2005, p. 88)

## Points of contact: Relativizing the Ego

In addition to the elaborate criticisms aimed at Jungian psychology, archetypal psychology has also adhered to and elaborated a significant amount of Jung's work. In fact, Hillman (2004) has noted: "It is without doubt that the first immediate father of archetypal psychology is Carl Gustav Jung" (p. 14). Whereas the points of contact are far too many to name and describe in this study, there are certain features of Jungian psychology that are central to archetypal theory and practice. Arguably the most salient of these connections is the work both Jung and Hillman have done to revision the dissociated and interiorized Cartesian subjectivity of the modern individual.

### The discovery of an interiorized subjectivity

In the seventeenth century Descartes crafted a philosophical position that has had wide-ranging psychological and theological implications throughout the Western world. For Descartes, each feature of the physical world was understandable in terms of bodies in motion. In an effort to please the Church, he proposed that God was the initial cause of motion (Gaukroger, 2006; van den Berg, 1961). Descartes argued: "As far as the general cause [of motion] is concerned, it seems obvious to me that this is none other than God himself, who, being omnipotent, in the beginning created matter with both motion and rest" (as cited in Garber, 1982, p. 166). Jan Hendrick Van den Berg (1961) has noted that Descartes' placement of God at the beginning of creation effectively abolished the primordial sense of God's immanence. With God removed from the immanent world, Descartes was free to investigate matter and self without concern for theological matters.

As God was sent forth from the realm of creation, the created world was reduced to objective reality, as defined by that which takes up space and is measurable, and subjective reality, as defined by a self-reflexive subject. Through these major shifts in cosmology, God became a distant abstract non-presence, and Friedrich Nietzsche's (1866/2001) proclamation that "God is dead" marks the moment when the distance became too great. Transcendence became absence, and absence became death.

This move had a profound effect on human consciousness. Paul Kugler (2005) commented:

> Prior to Descartes, existence was predicated on a transcendent God, Matter, or Eternal Forms. But with Descarte's *cogito ergo sum* "I think therefore I am"—the human subject for the first

> time is placed directly at the center of Western metaphysics and psychological understanding.
>
> (p. 67)

Descartes made an astounding cosmological move; he placed the human subject "at the center of our system of thought" (p. 67) and placed soul in the interior of the person.

### *The loss and recovery/discovery of the imaginal*

With Descartes' strict subject/object dualism, the space of in-between, the locale of soul since at least pre-Socratic Greek cosmology, was discarded—displaced in the massive transposition of God and subject. Cosmology collapsed into an ossified subject, separate and dead objects, and a far-away God. The angels of the imaginal, "the beings who connect us and keep us in touch with the glory and the wisdom of another order of reality" (Romanyshyn, 2002, p. 111) were cast off and deemed unnecessary. As Hillman (1975a) wrote, Cartesian psychology leaves "no space for anything intermediate, ambiguous, and metaphorical" (p. 1). He added: "This is a restrictive perspective and it has led us to believe that entities, other than human beings, taking on interior subjective qualities are merely 'anthropomorphized' or personified objects, not really persons in the accepted meaning of that word" (p. 1).

By the nineteenth century the subject had become so interiorized and isolated that there grew the essential need to bring this new structure of self into relation with the imaginal—a reestablishment of the self within the mythic cosmology. Prior to the development of the interiorized subject, this relationship was an inherent part of human identity. One communed with the Gods or God through ritual, prayer, and story. Jung (1956/1970) commented on the effect this separation has had on the modern individual: "One without a myth is like one uprooted, having no true link either with the past, or with the ancestral life which continues within him, or yet with contemporary human society" (p. 197). The isolated ego, torn from the pleroma,[2] became a symptom that required a response. Whereas Freud's psychology located a form of unconsciousness that was essentially sexual in response to the discarded sexuality of the Viennese Victorian social norm (Van den Berg, 1961), the type of unconsciousness located by Jung was mythical in nature, a "phylogenetically acquired unconscious peopled by mythic images" (Jung &

Shamdasani, 2009, p. 208), marked by the discarded relationship between the individual and the imaginal.

### *The birth of the imaginal ego*

Jung's self-experimentation described in his *Liber Novus* (also known as *The Red Book*), has provided a detailed documentation of his attempt to reconnect to the mythic unconscious (Jung & Shamdasani, 2009). Through the observations recorded in his diary, Jung ushered into the collective sphere both an ancient sensibility and a new way of relating to the imaginal. Because of the Cartesian split, which gave rise to the interiorizing of the subject and the birth of the modern ego, Jung was able to discover a radically new subject—an imaginal ego: a distinct but fluid sense of self, relativized by the multiple figures of the imaginal psyche.

The imaginal ego embodied a new capacity to relate to image with a metaphoric sensibility, as distinguished from rational modes of experiencing image, which, according to Jung, were limited to: artistic expression, philosophical speculation, a quasi-religious mode "leading to heresy and the founding of sects," and a squandering of image "in every form of licentiousness" (as cited in Jung & Shamdasani, 2009, p. 211). With Jung the spontaneous images of psyche became endowed with the wealth of inexhaustible metaphor. Furthermore, Jung recognized the importance of living one's life in close connection to this metaphoric sensibility.

Whereas positivistic science was quickly limiting human experience to the narrow confines of what is measurable and logical, Jung relativized the rational mind as merely one mode of approaching phenomena. Jung's imaginal dialogues played an important role in his process of differentiating rational and symbolic modes of experience. In an important dialogue recorded in Jung's *Black Book*, he recorded his soul as stating:

> "You know everything that is to be known about the manifested revelation, but you do not yet live everything that is to be lived at this time." Jung's "I" replied, "I can fully understand and accept this. However, it is dark to me, how the knowledge could be transformed into life. You must teach me this." His soul said, "There is not much to say about this. It is not as rational as you are inclined to think. The way is symbolic."
>
> (Jung & Shamdasani, 2009, p. 211)

Jung (1965) eventually concluded that the primary task was to come to terms with the unconscious through a rigorous endeavor of dialogue. He wrote: "I saw that so much fantasy needed firm ground underfoot, and that I must first return wholly to reality. . . . I had to draw concrete conclusions from the insights the unconscious had given me" (p. 188). It is this central undertaking that gave rise to Jung's psychological practices, particularly active imagination and dream analysis, which have come to form the heart of imaginal psychotherapy.

### *Image as ontologically real*

Jung's extensive work marks the birth of a modern epistemology that affords ontological status to psychic image not as a literal emanation from God but as an "as if" reality—a world that must be approached from a metaphoric sensibility, or what Jung called symbolic thinking. Western metaphysics since early Greek philosophy has stood with uncertainty in relation to psychic images, preferring the designations of imaginary, opinion, and epiphenomenon over the notion of imaginal or psychic reality (Kugler, 2005; Hillman, 1975b; Corbin, 1972). Alternatively, depth psychologists since the time of Jung have taken up radical defense of the imaginal as real and the real as imaginal (Romanyshyn, 2002). This sentiment is well captured in Robert Romanyshyn's declaration: "The imaginal is the grounding of the world; it has, therefore, ontological priority over the empirical and the rational" (p. 118).

This ontological position is central to both Jungian and archetypal psychology. As Shamdasani noted, "The notion that these figures had a psychological reality in their own right, and were not merely subjective figments, was the main lesson that he attributed to the fantasy figure of Elijah: psychic objectivity" (Jung & Shamdasani, 2009, p. 210). In his autobiography, Jung (1965) wrote the following: "Philemon and other figures of my fantasies brought home to me the crucial insight that there are things in the psyche which I do not produce, but which produce themselves and have their own life" (p. 183).

### *A second subjectivity*

With the shift towards valuing psychic image as primary rather than reproductive, the agency afforded to the Cartesian subject shifted, and a second subjective agency was discovered (Kugler, 2005). Kugler noted: "At the time, this was a radically new idea" (p. 70). Jung referred to this superordinate subjectivity as the self; as noted above, Hillman relies instead on the polytheistic notion of a pantheon of Gods. In either case, the ego is no longer the master of the house; it is the transpersonal imaginal subject, or subjects, that shape/s the now highly relativized and fluid ego. Jung (1942/1954) noted:

> The ego stands to the self as the moved to the mover, or as object to subject, because the determining factors which radiate out from the self surround the ego and are therefore supraordinate to it. . . . It is not I who creates myself, rather I happen to myself.
> (p. 155)

The imaginal ego is a receptive and curious devotee of psychic image, abiding in hospitality as a kind of "devotion to things as they are . . . [a] presence to the present moment which frees the image in the event, de-literalizes the factual character of the event, and dissolves preconceived ideas about what this moment is or should be" (Romanyshyn, 2002, p. 118).

Jung (1965) argued that the individual's development is contingent on a subjectivity that stands in close relation to the multiple emanations of the archetypal self. Hillman (1975a, 2007) echoes this essential attribute of the imaginal ego in his repeated admonishment to remember the Gods.

It is this relativizing (Hillman) or compensatory (Jung) function of the imaginal psyche that stands out as one of the most important contributions in the work of both Jung and Hillman. Descartes' reduction of the living world to measurable, controllable, and consumable resource has come with a heavy price. The imbalances in both psyche and matter are, needless to say, tremendous. Through the increasingly tight weave between ego and reason, imagination has become ego alien (Hillman, 1975b). The explication of the imaginal ego evidenced in the work of Jung and Hillman is both a remembrance of the essential place once afforded to soul as well as a new development aimed at forging an essential connection between the spirit of the time and the spirit of the depth (Jung & Shamdasani, 2009, p. 208).

## The question of clinical relevance

The various contributors to archetypal psychology have centered their work on the reflection of a new rhetoric for therapy and culture alike. The persistent attention to the epistemology of soul has resulted in an array of insights into the mercurial process of this oft-neglected aspect of being. However, the implications of these ideas remain largely untapped and dormant. Hillman's work has been considered by many clinical psychologists to be impractical and even irrelevant to the work they do with the suffering patient. Tacey (1998) has contended that Hillman has lost the "embodied reality of psychic life" (p. 218) to what he considered a philosophical head trip, invoked for its "rhetorical effect only" (p. 232).

As Tacey (1998) noted, rhetorical effect is indeed central to archetypal psychology. As a psychology rooted in aesthetics, the literature of archetypal psychology aims to evoke that which it describes, harking back to the ancient Greek's notion of the inseparability between truth and rhetoric—"rhetoric *qua* rhetoric reaches out to truth" (Grimaldi, 1978, p. 173).

Contrary to Tacey's heavy-handed critique, archetypal psychology carries an extensive collection of evocative ideas with a wealth of vital implications for the field of clinical psychology. With the focus on replacing the dominant fantasy of a scientific psychology with psychology as logos of soul, archetypal psychology has redefined the notion of therapy, shifting the focus from cure of the symptom to care of the soul (Hillman, 1972, 1975a, 1979a; Moore, 1994), an approach that is rooted in thinking psychologically about psychology. Clinical psychology, Hillman (1975a) argued, suffers from blindness to itself and a paucity of ideas. Countless textbooks, therapy manuals, and journal articles espouse a multitude of techniques for treating psychological malady, but few authors step back to see the ideas, or fantasies, that shape and determine the acclaimed technique. Alternatively, archetypal psychology has contributed a wealth of literature that effectively elucidates the archetypal determinants from which therapeutic practices emerge—a body of ideas that "engender the soul's reflection upon its nature, structure, and purpose" (Hillman, 1975a, p. 117).

The techniques of clinical psychology are often aimed at buffering the heroic ego against the diverse constituents of the psyche—coping, adaptation, development, growth, health, problem solving, all in service to the ego. In contrast to the predominant monocentric focus on ego adaptation, archetypal psychotherapy advocates for a polyphony of therapies to match the inherent multiplicity of the psyche. Each archetypal determinant is seen as having both a particular style of infirmity and a particular style of therapeutic method. The elucidation of these styles found in the literature of archetypal psychology may offer clinical psychology a broadening of concern beyond mere ego adaptation toward a therapy of archetypal significance.

Proponents of archetypal psychotherapy take a radical stance against mainstream psychology's strict adherence to the medical model (Hillman, 1975a, 1983; Paris, 2007; Romanyshyn, 2002). Reduction of symptoms, battling complexes, and strengthening ego are all moves away from one of the primary modes of soul expression: pathologizing. Hillman (1975a) wrote: "Before any attempt to treat, or even understand, pathologized phenomena we meet them in an act of faith, regarding them as authentic, real, and valuable *as they are*" (p. 75).

An archetypal approach to psychotherapy moves away from the notion of cure to the aim of vivification and seeing through of symptom and fantasy image. Pathology is redirected from the fantasy of treatment to a fantasy of poetics and fiction—highlighting the image's particularity and its metaphorical presence. While always sticking close to the image, one begins to see through its literal meanings to the mythopoetic undercurrent—an inexhaustible unfolding of metaphor and revelation.

In addition to abandoning the medical fantasy, archetypal psychology has also attempted to move away from Freud's leading fantasy that binds psyche to the early development of the child as well as Jung's fantasy of psychic oppositionalism (Hillman, 1975a, 2005). Hillman has posited that psychoanalysis has become stifled by the reification of these metaphors. The work of seeing through psychology itself helps shatter the intense identification with psychological schools and places psyche back on its natural grounds, which is, Hillman (1975a) argued, idiosyncratic expression of a polytheistic cosmos. Without the work of seeing through, psychology will "remain in a monotheistic model of consciousness which must be one-sided in its judgments and narrow in its vision, for it is unaware of the wealth and variety of psychological ideas" (p. 126).

## Notes

1 Radical: "a. Of, belonging to, or from a root or roots; fundamental to or inherent in the natural processes of life, vital; *spec.* designating the humour or moisture once thought to be present in all living organisms as a necessary condition of their vitality. b. Of a quality, attribute, or feature: inherent in the nature or essence of a person or thing; fundamental" (Radical, 2008).

2 Pleroma: "A state or condition of absolute fullness or plenitude; originally and chiefly that of God's being or identity" (Pleroma, 2008).

## References


Avens, R. (1980). *Imagination is reality: Western nirvana in Jung, Hillman, Barfield, and Cassirer* (Rev. ed.). Putnam, CT: Spring.

Berry, P. (1982). *Echo's subtle body: Contributions to an archetypal psychology.* Putnam, CT: Spring.

Berry, P. (1984). Jung's early psychiatric writing: The emergence of a psychopoetics (Unpublished Doctoral Dissertation). University of Dallas, Dallas, TX.

Berry, P. (2008). Rules of thumb towards an archetypal psychology practice. In S. Marlan (Ed.), *Archetypal psychologies: Reflections in honor of James Hillman* (pp. 327–340). New Orleans, LA: Spring Journal.

Bleakley, A. (1995). Animalizing and shamanizing: Animal presence in shamanism and archetypal psychology (Unpublished Doctoral Dissertation). University of Sussex, East Sussex, UK.

Casey, E. S. (1974). Toward a phenomenology of imagination. *The Journal of the British Society for Phenomenology, 5*(10), 29–52.

Conjunction. (2008). In *Oxford English dictionary online* (3rd ed.). Retrieved from www.oed.com.pgi.idm.oclc.org/view/Entry/39279?redirectedFrom=conjunction

Coppin, J. (1996). *Language in the Practice of Archetypal Psychotherapy* (Doctoral dissertation). Retrieved from ProQuest Digital Dissertations. (AAT 250069480)

Corbin, H. (1972). *Mundus imaginalis* or the imaginary and the imaginal. (R. Horine, Trans.). *Spring, 32*, pp. 1–13.

Edinger, E. F. (1992). *Ego and archetype.* Boston, MA: Shambhala.

Franz, M. V. (1996). *The interpretation of fairy tales* (Rev Sub.). Shambhala.

Garber, D. (1982). *Descartes embodied: Reading Cartesian philosophy through Cartesian science.* New York, NY: Cambridge University Press.

Gaukroger, S. (2006). *The emergence of a scientific culture: Science and the shaping of modernity 1210-1685.* New York, NY: Oxford University Press.

Giegerich, W. (1998). *The soul's logical life: towards a rigorous notion of psychology.* New York, NY: Peter Lang.

Goldenberg, N. (1975). Archetypal theory after Jung. *Spring*, 199–220.

Grimaldi, W. M. (1978). Rhetoric and truth: A note on Aristotle. *Philosophy & Rhetoric*, 11(3), 173–177.

Guggenbühl-Craig, A. (1971). *Power in the helping professions.* New York, NY: Continuum International.

Hartman, J. V. (1980). Psychotherapy: An attempt at a definition. *Spring, 47*, 90–100.

Hillman, J. (1970). Why 'archetypal' psychology? *Spring, 30*, 212–219.

Hillman, J. (1971). Psychology: Monotheistic or polytheistic. *Spring, 31*, 193–207.

Hillman, J. (1972). *The myth of analysis.* Evanston: Northwestern University Press.

Hillman, J. (1975a). *Re-visioning psychology.* New York, NY: Harper and Row.

Hillman, J. (1975b). *Loose ends: Primary papers in archetypal psychology.* Putnam, CT: Spring.

Hillman, J. (1977a). An inquiry into image. *Spring, 44*, 62–88.

Hillman, J. (1977b). Notes for an inquiry into image. [Unpublished notes]. The James Hillman Collection (D77a, 2.1). OPUS Archives and Research Center, Carpinteria, CA.

Hillman, J. (1978). Further notes on images. *Spring*, *45*, 152–182.

Hillman, J. (1979a). *Dream and underworld*. New York, NY: Harper and Row.

Hillman, J. (1979b). Image-sense. *Spring*, *46*, 130–143.

Hillman, J. (1980). The therapeutic value of alchemical language. In I. F. Baker (Ed.), *Methods of treatment in analytical psychology* (pp. 118–126). Fellvack: Bonz.

Hillman, J. (1983). *Healing fiction*. Berrytown, New York: Station Hill Press.

Hillman, J. (1991). *Inter views: conversations with Laura Pozzo on psychotherapy, biography, love, soul, dreams, work, imagination, and the state of the culture.* Putnam, CT: Spring.

Hillman, J. (1992). *The thought of the heart and the soul of the world*. Putnam, CT: Spring Publications, Inc.

Hillman, J. (Speaker). (1993). *In Defense of Melancholy*. [Cassette Recording, No. 1–7]. Santa Barbara, CA: Pacifica Graduate Institute.

Hillman, J. (1997). *The souls code: In search of character and calling*. New York, NY: Grand Central.

Hillman, J. (Speaker). (1999). *The Work of C.G. Jung: Reflections on its Roots, Branches, and Buds*. [Cassette Recording, 1–6]. Santa Barbara, CA: Pacifica Graduate Institute.

Hillman, J. (2004). *Archetypal psychology*. Putnam, CT: Spring.

Hillman, J. (2005). *Senex and puer*. Putnam, CT: Spring.

Hillman, J. (2007). *Mythic figures*. Putnam, CT: Spring.

Jung, C. G. (1954). Foreword to Suzuki's introduction to Zen Buddhism. In H. Read, M. Fordham, G. Adler, & W. McGuire (Eds.), *The collected works of C. G. Jung* (R. F. C. Hull, Trans.) (Vol. 11, pp. 538–557). Princeton, NJ: Princeton University Press. (Original work published 1939)

Jung, C. G. (1954). A psychological approach to the dogma of the trinity. In H. Read, M. Fordham, G. Adler, & W. McGuire (Eds.), *The collected works of C. G. Jung* (R. F. C. Hull, Trans.) (Vol. 11, pp. 107–200). Princeton, NJ: Princeton University Press. (Original work published 1942)

Jung, C. G. (1960). The real and the surreal. In H. Read, M. Fordham, G. Adler, & W. McGuire (Eds.), *The collected works of C. G. Jung* (R. F. C. Hull, Trans.) (Vol. 8, pp. 382–384). Princeton, NJ: Princeton University Press. (Original work published 1933)

Jung, C. G. (1964). *Man and his symbols*. New York, NY: Dell.

Jung, C. G. (1965). *Memories, dreams, reflections*. New York, NY: Vintage Books.

Jung, C. G. (1966). The practical use of dream analysis. In H. Read, M. Fordham, G. Adler, & W. McGuire (Eds.), *The collected works of C. G. Jung* (R. F. C. Hull, Trans.) (Vol. 16, pp. 139–161). Princeton, NJ: Princeton University Press. (Original work published 1934)

Jung, C. G. (1967). Symbols of transformation. In H. Read, M. Fordham, G. Adler, & W. McGuire (Eds.), *The collected works of C. G. Jung* (R. F. C. Hull, Trans.) (2nd ed., Vol. 5). Princeton, NJ: Princeton University Press. (Original work published 1912)

Jung, C. G. (1968). Commentary on the secret of the golden flower. In H. Read, M. Fordham, G. Adler, & W. McGuire (Eds.), *The collected works of C. G. Jung* (R. F. C. Hull, Trans.) (Vol. 13, pp. 1–56). Princeton, NJ: Princeton University Press. (Original work published 1929)

Jung, C. G. (1968). Introduction to the religious and psychological problems of alchemy. In H. Read, M. Fordham, G. Adler, & W. McGuire (Eds.), *The collected works of C. G. Jung* (R. F. C. Hull, Trans.) (2nd ed., Vol. 12, pp. 12–101). Princeton, NJ: Princeton University Press. (Original work published 1936)

Jung, C. G. (1968). Individual dream symbolism in relation to alchemy. In H. Read, M. Fordham, G. Adler, & W. McGuire (Eds.), *The collected works of C. G. Jung* (R. F. C. Hull, Trans.) (2nd ed., Vol. 12, pp. 102–223). Princeton, NJ: Princeton University Press. (Original work published 1937)

Jung, C. G. (1968). Aion. In H. Read, M. Fordham, G. Adler, & W. McGuire (Eds.), *The collected works of C. G. Jung* (R. F. C. Hull, Trans.) (Vol. 9ii). Princeton, NJ: Princeton University Press. (Original work published 1951)

Jung, C. G. (1969). Concerning rebirth. In H. Read, M. Fordham, G. Adler, & W. McGuire (Eds.), *The collected works of C. G. Jung* (R. F. C. Hull, Trans.) (Vol. 9i, pp. 113–150). Princeton, NJ: Princeton University Press. (Original work published 1950)

Jung, C. G. (1970). Mysterium coniunctionis: An inquiry into the separation and synthesis of psychic opposites in alchemy. In H. Read, M. Fordham, G. Adler, & W. McGuire (Eds.), *The collected works of C. G. Jung* (R. F. C. Hull, Trans.) (2nd ed., Vol. 14). Princeton, NJ: Princeton University Press. (Original work published 1956)

Jung, C. G. (1970). On the nature of the psyche. In H. Read, M. Fordham, G. Adler, & W. McGuire (Eds.), *The collected works of C. G. Jung* (R. F. C. Hull, Trans.) (Vol. 8, pp. 159–236). Princeton, NJ: Princeton University Press. (Original work published 1947)

Jung, C. G., & Shamdasani, S. (2009). *Liber novus*. New York, NY: W.W. Norton & Co.

Keats, J. (2001). *Complete poems and selected letters of John Keats*. New York, NY: Random House Digital. (Original work published 1899)

Kugler, P. (2005). *Raids on the unthinkable: Freudian and Jungian psychoanalyses*. New Orleans, LA: Spring Journal.

Lopez-Pedraza, R. (1977). *Hermes and his children*. Zurich, Switzerland: Spring.

Moore, T. (1994). *Care of the soul: A guide for cultivating depth and sacredness in everyday life*. New York, NY: Harper Perennial.

Neumann, E. (1995). *The origins and history of consciousness*. Princeton, NJ: Princeton University Press. (Original work published 1954)

Newman, K. D. (1980). Counter-transference and consciousness. *Spring*, *47*, 117–127.

Nietzsche, F. W. (2001). *The gay science: With a prelude in German rhymes and an appendix of songs*. (B. A .O. Williams & J. Nauckhoff, Trans.). New York, NY: Cambridge University Press. (Original work published 1866)

Paris, G. (2007). *Wisdom of the psyche: Depth psychology after neuroscience*. New York, NY: Routledge.

Pleroma. (2008). In *Oxford English dictionary online* (3rd ed.), Retrieved from www.oed.com.pgi.idm.oclc.org/view/Entry/145726?redirectedFrom=pleroma#eid

Romanyshyn, R. (2002). *Ways of the heart: Essays toward an imaginal psychology*. Pittsburgh, PA: Trivium Publications.
Russell, D. (2013). *The life and ideas of James Hillman: The making of a psychologist* Vol. 1). New York, NY: Helios Press.
Samuels, A. (1985). *Jung and the post-Jungians*. New York, NY: Routledge.
Schenk, R. (1989). The soul of beauty: A psychological investigation of appearance (Unpublished Doctoral Dissertation). University of Dallas, Dallas, TX.
Schenk, R. (2001). *The sunken quest, the wasted fisher, the pregnant fish: Postmodern reflections on depth psychology*. Wilmette, IL: Chiron.
Tacey, D. (1997). *Remaking men: Jung, spirituality and social change*. London: Routledge.
Tacey, D. (1998). Twisting and turning with James Hillman: From anima to world soul, from academia to pop. In A. Casement (Ed.) *Post-Jungians today: Key papers in contemporary analytical psychology*. New York, NY: Routledge.
Tacey, D. (2001). *Jung and the New Age*. Philadelphia, PA: Brunner-Routledge.
Van den Berg, J. H. (1961). *The changing nature of man*. (H. F. Croes, Trans.). New York, NY: Dell.
Vannoy-Adams, M. (2008). The archetypal school. In P. Young-Eisendrath & T. Dawson (Eds.). *The Cambridge companion to Jung* (2nd edn, pp. 107–124). New York, NY: Cambridge University Press.
Watkins, M. (1981). Six approaches to the image in art therapy. *Spring*, *48*, 107–125.
Watkins, M. (1984). *Waking dreams*. Dallas, TX: Spring.
Watkins, M. (1986). *Invisible guests: The development of imaginal dialogues*. Dallas, TX: Spring.

Chapter 2

# Imaginal practice

## Beginning with image

Standing in a crowded forest, sight is obscured except for where the trees open out to the horizon. The light coming in through the clearing discloses a certain perspective and casts shadows over other images.[1] Here, in the space of interpretive vision, we find ourselves always already situated within a perspective. We have in hand both definitions and formulations. Drawn forward by the call of the clearing, we begin on a path, a method of investigation that both reveals and conceals. The position taken gives way to a particular style of interpretation while simultaneously covering over alternate paths of investigation. Caught by habits, the well-worn path, we lose the shadows, the surprise of unfettered imagination.

Following Jung's (1939/1954a) argument that "every psychic process is an image and an 'imagining"' (p. 544), archetypal psychology has established itself as a psychology that abstains from habits, beginning instead with the image; whether in dream, fantasy, symptom, or event, all psychic events are treated as imaginal, that is metaphorical, expressive of meaning through aesthetic display, and rife with a fecundity of meaning. In relating to the psyche vis-à-vis image, one takes a stance in a perspective that is polycentric, many-centered. Beginning with image is like being in a forest where the winding path leads through a multitude of clearings—each disclosing a view and a path that had been hitherto unknown. The image reveals, and then, in a mercurial fashion, shifts to a different center, displaying aspects of that which had been concealed in an enigmatic cascade of meaning. "The true iconoclast is the image" (Hillman, 1975a, p. 8) as it continually breaks itself and begins again.

Whereas symbols (phallus, breast, water) are, by definition, generalized renditions, a composite of collective experience, images (looking up at a towering skyscraper, laying down on a grassy round hill, stepping into a fast-flowing cold-as-ice river) are always, as Hillman has noted, "particularized by a specific context, mood, and scene . . . they are precisely qualified" (Hillman, 1977, p. 62). Precision results in differentiation, which is, according to Jung, the bread and butter of individuation. Reading an event for its symbolic content trades the actual psychological phenomenon, full of idiosyncratic and highly differentiated meaning, for a reified abstraction wiped clean of the psyche from which it was made. Interpretations become indoctrination, nudging the individual to think in line with the preferred hermeneutic. No surprises, only rotted names.

Following Jung, Hillman (2004) has recognized image as the primary datum of psyche, "the governing fantasy by means of which consciousness is possible to begin with" (p. 24). Hillman has argued that image-making, *poésis*, is the "self-generative activity of the soul itself" (p. 18). The soul continuously weaves images into fantasy and dream, and these mythopoetic images, Hillman (1972) affirmed, are the foundational basis of human experience—a notion that connects back to Aristotle's claim that no thought occurs without an image.

Take for example the ringing of an alarm clock on a particularly drowsy morning. The sound takes shape in one's field of awareness, and as soon as it is registered it finds its expression as dream. My own alarm clock, which is a recording of a bell tower ringing, has expressed itself in dream as a school bell dismissing me from my eighth grade class as well as church bells ringing off in the distance. This propensity toward image-making is ubiquitous.

A second example arrives by way of politics. On July 13, 2012, President Barack Obama made the following remark at a campaign event in Roanoke, Virginia:

> If you were successful, somebody along the line gave you some help. There was a great teacher somewhere in your life. Somebody helped to create this unbelievable American system that we have that allowed you to thrive. Somebody invested in roads and bridges. If you've got a business—you didn't build that. Somebody else made that happen.

Subsequently, the media, particularly conservative news stations like Fox News exploded with response to one phrase, "you didn't build that." Ripped from its presenting context, phrase became image and was woven into the republican mythos of individualism and free enterprise. Deepening into the image, one finds a complete narrative based on a literalized fantasy that has been inculcated into the people through media and campaign rhetoric, a collective complex rife with affect, psychologically primitive defenses, and a kind of ideological obstinacy that has helped usher the United States into political gridlock and an array of social, economic, and religious crises: soaring unemployment, a devastating recession, house foreclosures, religious warfare, hate crimes, and so on.

We are all subject to falling into the grip of these images, subject to monocentric perspectives and narrow-minded actions. However, once the image is freed from the hard crust of literalism, it discloses itself as perspectival, metaphorical, affectively laden, and determined—actually overdetermined—by personal psychodynamics, social constructions, and archetypal patterns. For better or worse, this image-making is a constant phenomena—sensory input, emotions, thoughts, all arise out of and return to an underlying imaginal matrix. We simply cannot have experience outside of our culturally-historically situated image-making capacity. However, we can, according to Jung, develop some psychological flexibility in relation to these cultural complexes by "reconciling the spirit of the time with the spirit of the depth" (Jung & Shamdasani, 2009, p. 208), fostering dialogue between the mythopoetic imagination, our collective history, and the more narrow view of ego consciousness.

Jung's (1921/1971) central focus throughout his life was to explicate the phenomenology of this mythopoetic matrix, which he called *esse in anima*, a psychic reality that abides as a mediating space between the physical, *esse in re*, and the intellectual, *esse in intellectu*. Jung noted: "Only through the specific vital activity of the psyche does the sense-impression attain that intensity, and the idea that effective force, which are the two indispensable constituents of living reality" (p. 52). Image offers intensity and effective force. In other words, image evokes the emotional stimulation that ties each of us to life.

As Berry (1984) argued, this third position of imagination, located as a mediating force between idea and matter, is a place of creative activity, an aesthetic making, that "creates reality everyday" (Jung, 1921/1971, p. 52). Berry (1984) made the following point:

> Since *esse in anima* is a midpoint between subjective and objective, imaginative and material, inner and outer, fantasy and

> reality, it shares something of the nature of each but in a new nonliteral form, which Jung calls "images." Images are the vehicles of psychological reality.
>
> (p. 124)

From the intermediary position of image, the distinctions between internal and external become irrelevant. Image transcends or rather dissolves the strictures of Cartesian boundaries. Image, like emotion, is always related to both inner and outer experience. Contemporary psychoanalysis has described this space of mediation as the intersubjective nature of the psyche—we are always in a relational experience (Stolorow, Brandchaft, & Atwood, 1987). Even an experience of isolation and aloneness is one part of a relationship (R. D. Stolorow, personal communication, May 18, 2012).

## *Image and affect*

Whereas both imaginal and affective phenomena have value unto themselves, therapeutic method generally favors feelings while neglecting the imaginal, which, Hillman (2004) argued, ultimately results in bolstering the habitual position of the ego. He wrote: "The intensified singleness that emotions bring, their narrowing moncentristic effect upon consciousness, gives support to the already monotheistic tendency of the ego to appropriate and identify with its experiences" (p. 59). Disregard of the imaginal layer of one's emotional experience tends to result in an inflexible identification with the feeling as the totality of experience, as opposed to one face of a complex phenomenon. The feeling is treated as literal and unequivocal. The "I" in I am sad, or I am angry, is a swollen "I," an "I" that has gobbled up all the other imaginal figures present in the emotion, resulting in an undifferentiated imagination and an overburdened ego.

As a polyvalent and phenomenological psychology, archetypal psychotherapy is interested in both the multiple faces of an experience as well as the particularity of each face. Descriptors like anger, sadness, fear, and joy are all broad and general—dead words that do little to differentiate one's experience. An image, as I have noted, is always particular. When anger is qualified by an image, one gains a wealth of material with which to work.

For example, one patient noted that he was feeling angry. He went on to describe how when he walks through a wealthy neighborhood and sees an expensive car he wants to smash the window or slash the tires. His anger was qualified by destruction, or rather destruction is the anger: a smashing-glass-cutting-rubber-anger. A subsequent therapeutic move might entail exploring this image as metaphor. In tracking the interrelation of the image, one could extrapolate that he shifts quickly from anger to envy to the destruction of valued material. One might take up the way in which the image offers a disclosure of the patient's response to his socio-economic situation. His anger is, at least partially, a reply to his position in an economic hierarchy where he is separated from prosperity by a transparent barrier, tantalized by the wealth on the other side. How else does his anger smash and cut that which has value? Intimate relationships? Personal successes? Family memories? How do these experiences leave him with deflated tires, broken windows, and bleeding fists? One might think of this dynamic in terms of the transference. In what ways might he destroy the value fostered throughout the treatment, or how might he break through the glass window of neutrality between he and I in order to bring us to the same level—broken, angry, destroyed?

The image of smashing glass and slashing tires arrived alongside, fed into, and helped differentiate, the always already present image of presentation. This patient was already disclosing images of his anger with gesture, tone, breath, and cadence. Whereas psychoanalytic technique attends to presentation as derivative material, interpreting these expressions as pointing to a central image—transference, archetypal psychology flips this notion on its head, arguing that the gesture, tone, breath, and cadence are the central image, are the transference. Presentation *is* meaning.

The embodied response to this kind of imaginal therapy is a psychological action that undercuts literalism and the destructive acts to which literalism gives rise. The window of the expensive car becomes an imaginal window through which the patient has the opportunity to catch bits of soul-in-the-world. The anger-filled walk through the rich neighborhood is transmuted into a place where psyche is on the surface, meaning and materiality meet.

A dream:

> *I was standing by myself at an elevator door. A group of intimidating looking guys approached me. One of them had three darts in his hand. He showed me the back end of the darts, the flight—a part of the dart that stabilizes its trajectory. He challenged me to fight him with the darts. Terrified by the situation, I refused.*

> *He continued to pressure me, and eventually I took hold of the darts. While standing very close, he began throwing his darts at my body. I used my left hand and arm to deflect the attack. However, I was still getting hit. The group of guys made a comment indicating I shouldn't try to defend myself. Suddenly, without thinking, I swung my right hand at the man's neck and stabbed his jugular vein with my dart. I took a moment to move it around, trying to make the cut bigger. Then I ran.*

The dream provides a constellation of emotion: intimidating fear, defensiveness, murderous rage, and a return to fear. However, simply extrapolating this pattern of emotion leaves significant portions of the image behind.

In the particular details of the image, I find the dream highlighting the relationship between feeling attacked and standing by myself in my standing pattern of elevating (into my intellect; away from aggressive feelings). The dream also demonstrates a dart-like precision in my aggression; the way in which I present myself like a dart board, my bull's eye exposed; the sudden quality of my anger; the way I dart from my anger and take flight; the way I snap and go for the jugular, then run like hell.

The dream underscores the linking of aggression and flight through repetition in the language of the dream, using words like "cut" and "run," which is a phrase soldiers have used to describe a cowardly retreat. The dream also makes a link between fight, flight, and stabilization, evoking questions about the de-stabilized nature of my response to aggression—is the way I take flight from a fight wild and without direct trajectory?

The dream asks many questions and opens many doors—different aspects revealed with each return. Each move made with the image is a completion, and every ending evokes another beginning, fostering an ever-deepening relationship. This mode of imaginal reflection, rife with a seemingly limitless variety of conclusions,[2] should be clearly differentiated from modes of interpretation that replace these conclusions with stoppings. Too often interpretations rely on what is known, cauterizing the imaginal experience into one particular narrative. By keeping to the image, we keep close to what is unknown, allowing that which has been interpretively uncovered to die to the continual procession of beginnings.

Engagement with the images of dream and fantasy, however, can also usher in a sense of psychological organization—an imaginal topography by which one can orient to psychic reality. In his autobiography, Jung (1965) described the way in which he used image to manage the onslaught of emotion he experienced during a profoundly volatile time in his life. He noted:

> To the extent that I managed to translate the emotions into image—that is to say, to find the images which were concealed in the emotions—I was inwardly calmed and reassured. Had I left those images hidden in the emotions, I might have been torn to pieces by them. There is a chance that I might have succeeded in splitting them off; but in that case I would inexorably have fallen into a neurosis and so been ultimately destroyed by them anyhow. (p. 177)

Jung, as an old man after many years of working with the psyche, suggested that if the image remained latent in the emotion, he would have been torn to pieces or fallen into a neurosis, implying that neurosis is linked with a failure of imagination. When imagination becomes monocentric, evoking a rigid identification with one perspective, like the "you didn't build it" fiasco, the individual or culture becomes subject to a kind of pathological relation to self and world.

The capacity to imagine, that is the ability to relate to the constellation of image associated with one's emotional experience, is central in Jung's formulation of psychological health. Jung does not stand alone in this claim. The authors of the *Psychodynamic Diagnostic Manual* have listed as one of nine central features that comprise psychological functioning "the capacity to form internal representations," which they describe as "the individual's capacity to symbolize affectively meaningful experience (that is, to organize experience in a mental, rather than somatic or behavioral form)" (PDM Task Force, 2006, p. 73).

Despite the agreement upon the importance of symbolic capacity, the way in which these images or internal representations are understood varies widely among both Freudian and Jungian branches of psychoanalysis. One central difference can be traced back to a primary disagreement between Jung and Freud. As Berry (1984) noted:

> Unlike Freud, Jung views the psyche's images not as deriving from events or hallucinated wish fulfillments but rather as images in their own right, images of a psychic imagination whose intentions are distinct from the personal ego's wishes or concerns. (p. 14)

From Jung's perspective, the image is impersonal, and the emotion is the claim it has made on the individual. As such, emotions, as well as symptoms, are not simply experiences to be resolved or sublimated, but also require imaginal responsivity and relationship.

Emotions provoke action. Underneath the emotion, underneath every emotion, is a fantasy. What one does with the emotion is, from a psychological perspective, secondary in significance to understanding the fantasy that is pushing the experience. Which psychic character is calling for attention? When this question finds its answer, the emotion becomes relativized and qualified by the image, and the individual has an opportunity to step outside the grip of the fantasy and move towards a psychologically informed action—an action that begins with psyche.

This type of psychological relating is well depicted in Jung's relationship with Philemon.[3] Jung (1965) noted:

> Through him the distinction was clarified between myself and the object of my thought. He confronted me in an objective manner, and I understood that there is something in me which can say things that I do not know and do not intend, things which may even be directed against me.
>
> (p. 183)

Although Jung's relationship with Philemon was rather congenial, his statement acknowledges the important observation that psychic images are in no way benign. Just as Freud (1920/1975) recognized a function of the psyche that is fundamentally anti-life, Jung's encounter with the unconscious taught him that images can be both wise consults, like Philemon, as well as something more akin to demonic possession—images that are fueled by an aggressive drive turned against the ego.

This distinction is often unrecognized or underemphasized in the literature of archetypal psychology, where image is most often elevated above and superior to the needs of the ego. Describing the relationship between ego and image, Hillman (1975a) noted: "The ego enters their realm at first as a stalker, then as their pupil, finally as their maintenance man, performing small adjustments, keeping the building in repair, the fires stoked, warming" (p. 41).

Throughout Hillman's (1975a) writing he has presented an argument, both persuasive and necessary, for the need to relativize "the habitual modes of experiencing with which we are so identified that they are called ego, I" (p. 43); however, his argument often fails to consider those instances in which the image would be better served by a fantasy of the I-image taking a stand in relation to a brutally oppressive and destructive force. An unequivocally subservient relationship to image is not only dangerous but also inhibiting of the necessary tension required between the ego and the image.

### Relating to images

The relational tension that forms between ego and image does not necessarily need to be verbal. As Mary Watkins (1984) noted, "each image discloses its own character—the particular way it shapes and expresses the nature of the imaginal—by being itself. It tells what it is doing by doing it, by acting itself out" (p. 99). The image defines itself through its presentation and movements. This important point reminds the practitioner of the patience and observation necessary to imaginal work and prevents the individual from interrogating the image. Relating to the image requires an awakening of one's sense perception vis-à-vis the unique particularity of the phenomena at hand. However, as Hillman (1979b) has observed, the senses, once adapted to the imaginal, lose the boundaries set by the literal and take on the more fluid quality of metaphor, "so that we can 'read an image,' as Lopez-Pedraza says, and 'hear psyche speaking,' as Robert Sardello says" (p. 131).

Just as one attends to the particular expression of the image, it is also important to notice the particular style of consciousness to which one is identified while engaging the image. The ego has many faces, each of which is archetypally constituted. Psychologizing, or seeing through, to the underlying style may free the individual from a rigidified stance in relation to the image. Most notably, the heroic ego tends to suffocate the image with literalism and exploitation—as Watkins (1986) wrote, "this kind of heroic ego enters the imaginal but often for its own gain and in order to return to its usual kingdom richer and wiser than ever" (p. 116).

### Relativizing the hero

Archetypal psychology has often aimed its sharp sword of critique at the throat of the hero, attempting to free imaginal psychology from the rote determination and limitation of this style of consciousness. Perhaps, embedded in this stance, has been a bit of the hero himself.

Like cures like—the hero must ultimately use his heroic force to restrain himself from action.

Imaginal work is rife with the unknown, the mysterious, the surprising. When faced with the unknown, the heroic style of response is to conquer. Through conquest, the hero not only absolves himself of the anxiety fostered by the unknown, but also, as seen in numerous fairy tales and myths, gains the esteem, endorsement, and reward of the civilized world.

Like the distressed townsfolk who have been tormented by the attacking dragon, those enduring a suffering of the soul want an equally strong and opposing force to quell the suffering—a hero to slay the dragon. The pull to offer some immediate relief is a tenacious temptation throughout treatment. To complicate matters, this pull comes not only from the patient. The therapist's heroic desire is often close at hand, offering an interpretation or some other gesture in hopes of maintaining a sense of efficacy.

This style of response drains the vitality of the image. As Hillman (1979a) noted, when the mighty Hercules pays visit to the underworld, he pulls his sword and injures Hades. When faced with death, the hero responds with violence: "Rather than die to metaphor, we kill literally; refusing the need to die, we attack death itself" (p. 110).

Berry (1982) qualified this style of consciousness as "that mode which severs the inherent continuity and intraconnection of the dream image as a whole" (p. 68). She added:

> This mode continuously makes divisions between good and bad, friends and enemies, positive and negative, in accord with how well these figures and events comply with our notion of progression. Then to interpret as "negative" or "positive" these same characters is to take the narrative at face value, thereby getting caught in the dream ego's idea of movement.
>
> (p. 68)

This observation contains immeasurable importance for an archetypal approach to psychotherapy. The pull towards heroic action is clearly a form of resistance to the psychological expression of the image, its ego-dystonic nature, and the further the image is from one's habitual mode of fantasy, the stronger the desire to reshape it.

As such, the personal associations one produces in relation to an image are approached as secondary expressions and may often do more for qualifying the ego's perspective towards the image than the image itself (Berry, 1982, p. 70). It is as if personal associations and elaborations contextualize the ego in the particular constellation or imaginal relationship. However, the image, as noted above, arrives with its own context. A primary aim in working a dream from an imaginal perspective is to clearly differentiate and hold in tension the suppositions of both the dream ego and waking ego, as well as the essential qualities of the image. When attention is afforded to both the imaginal and ego positions, the fixity of consciousness loosens, allowing more psychological fluidity.

Berry (1982) has offered an important guideline to which one might adhere, and in so doing, limit the reductionism and monocentrism of heroic consciousness. This guideline, which she has referred to as "Layard's rule," states: "*Nothing in the dream is wrong, except perhaps the dream ego*" (p. 83). Hillman (1979a) expressed a similar notion when describing one of the primary principles of archetypal dream work: conservation. He noted, "Conservation implies holding on to what is and even assuming that what is is right" (p. 117).

Take, for example, the following dream:

> *I am standing on the driveway of my mother's house looking at the rear-end of my father's car. Half of it, the driver's side has no ground underneath it. Apparently, the drive way has been dug up. I feel very anxious about the car tipping into the hole; however I am also aware that if I were to get into the driver's seat to move it onto a safe space, my weight would surely tip it over into the abyss.*

In considering this dream from the perspective of Layard's Rule, the images quickly disclose different valences, evoking thoughts about groundlessness and the importance of letting things fall. Stepping outside the anxious perspective of the dream ego, we may begin to imagine that it is essential for the car, that which I drive or that which drives me, to teeter on the edge, always ready to plummet into the unknown, the unexpected, where the drives are thwarted, confused, turned upside down.

## *Imaginal ego*

As this mode of relating to the image becomes internalized, one begins to gain access to a style of consciousness characterized by an active relationship to image and death, where death means the loss of all dayworld conceptions, a perspective shaped by Hades: "receiving, hospitable yet relentlessly deepening, attuned to the nocturne, dusky, and with a fearful cold intelligence that gives permanent shelter in his house to the incurable conditions of human being" (Hillman, 1979a, p. 202). The ego throws down its favored weapons of rationality, positivistic knowing, causality, literalism, strength, and growth. Like Cerberus guarding the gates of the underworld, the imaginal ego protects the image from the battalions of reduction led by the anxiety-fueled force of literalism.

Hillman (1979a) has noted that the move away from literalism requires a de-christianizing of the image, reversing the prohibition against the freedom of imagination, a prohibition that, for example, makes no distinction between the fantasy of adultery and the flesh and blood act, precluding awareness of all the metaphorical implications of an adulterous fantasy. Alternatively, in upholding a metaphorical sensibility, granting imagination its autonomy, the energy of the ego, no longer directed towards the constant reinforcement of the defensive walls, can instead wonder about why this image. What are its implications?

Watkins (1986) has described various stages of development one might pass through as he or she begins to relate to the imaginal—moving from the imaginal other as an extension of the ego to embodying a clearly differentiated autonomy. She noted as the ego is seen as relative to a retinue of diverse voices "truth becomes redefined. It is not the province of a single voice, but arises between the voices at the interface of the characters' multiple perspectives" (p. 121). Watkins has argued for the development of an ego that can function as a narrator in a novel would function—a "hermetic go-between to the multiple voices one encounters" (p. 128). The perspective of the ego develops from a fantasy of omniscience in relation to the various psychological happenings to an understanding that must develop through a dialogue, "which preserves the integrity of both self and other" (p. 128), an I–thou relationship.

Hillman (1975a) has described this type of image-making as personifying. He noted "personifying is a way of being in the world and *experiencing the world as a psychological field*, where persons are given with events, so that events are experiences that touch us, move us, appeal to us" (p. 13). Personifying shifts the focus from the rational/analytical questions of why and how to the imaginal question of who. Locating the who in an experience fosters relationship with one's world "so that we can find access to them with our hearts" (p. 14).

### *Instinct and image*

Hillman's emphasis on personifying as one of the primary modes of soul-making is in close allegiance with the psychopoetic strands running through the work of both Freud and Jung. Although Freud attempted to frame psychoanalysis as a discipline of science, he was also clearly aware of the mythic aspect of the psyche. In Freud's (1920/1975) essay *Beyond the Pleasure Principle* he began to use the term Eros to describe libidinal instinct. This move connected the central feature of his psychology with the longstanding mythopoetic tradition surrounding this figure. In a similar spirit, Freud noted "Instincts are mythical beings, superb in their indefiniteness" (Freud, 1933/1964, p. 118).

Jung also described the connection between instinct and the polyphony of psychic characters. Jung (1939/1954b) placed image as the primary psychic phenomena, noting "nothing can be known unless it first appears as a psychic image" (p. 480). In addition, he (1933/1960) asserted: "We may say that the image represents the meaning of the instinct" (p. 204). According to Jung, we can only experience instinct as image. Aggression and sexuality always appear as personified figures of some sort, and the way in which they appear, their aesthetic presentation is representative of their meaning.

The shift in emphasis from instinct to image carries with it a shift in therapeutic action. Interpretive comments that aim at elucidating various instinctual derivatives and affects miss the more experience-near and precisely qualified effect of the image. Moreover, following Jung's assertion that the image holds the meaning of the instinct, a failure to fully differentiate the image results in a failure to fully differentiate the meaning of the instinctual expression. The qualification that the image would have provided is replaced with conceptual speculation by therapist and patient.

### *The nature of image*

An archetypal approach to image is distinct from Jung's approach in that Jung posited a distinction between a virtual or *a priori* image, consistent with his notion of the archetype, and the archetypal image. One can only infer the virtual image from the archetypal image since the virtual image is not available to experience. This is similar to Freud's (1900/1953) manifest and latent content, except in Jung the latent dream thought would be of archetypal significance. Alternatively, Hillman (1977) and Berry (1984) have argued for a psychopoetic approach to the image in which one is only concerned with what has been presented—the manifest content—"the image as phenomenally immediate" (Berry, 1984, p. 131).

Archetypal psychology posits that an image is different from an internal object in that the latter is a derivative of the former. Phenomenologically, the individual experiences the dream as prior. Then suppositions are made in regards to what the image refers (that is, an internalized mother imago). Although the image is *analogous* to the concept of internal object, it is in no way equal or reducible to this particular conceptual formulation.

In addition, the notion of image is not limited to that which can be visually perceived. An image can be a turn of phrase, a smell, a taste, a touch; even "language itself is . . . an image" (Jung, 1939/1959, p. 160). Casey (1974) has argued that image is a mode of approaching phenomena. Berry (1984) offered the following clarification:

> The image may be a particular entity in a dream or a configuration in the dream, the dream in its entirety, the dream within a situation, symptom, the course of an illness, etc. The image is simply that upon which the work of crafting focuses as given and nonnegotiable.
>
> (p. 156)

### *Archetypal interpretation*

As noted above, archetypal psychology has put forth strong critiques of interpretive methods that move away from the presenting phenomena. Alternatively Berry (1984) has imagined the interpretive act as an aesthetic craft that is mimetic to the way the psyche crafts images from nature. The aesthetic approach has been cogently described by Berry (1984) as "grounding in the immediate sensuous details of what presents itself," implying "distinct actualities, leading to descriptions rather than to secondary rationalizations about descriptions" (p. 69).

The psyche's work is a *poésis*, weaving day residues, distant memories, and the activation of intrapsychic structures into a particular type of psychological making, an image. Similarly, an archetypal approach to interpreting psychic phenomena aims at an "affective connaturality" or an "attitude of correspondences" (Berry, 1984, p. 151) with the particular image. Instead of formulating an interpretation from one's intellectual grasp of psychological concepts, the interpretation stems from an aesthetic sensibility. As Ronald Schenk (1989) noted, "no systems of proportion, harmony, oppositions or compensation are called for in order to elucidate meaning. Appearance itself is all that is necessary when perceived through the aesthetic eye" (p. 161). The meaning is derived not from a preconception of a source of meaning, but from aesthetic principles, "by way of similarities, reverberations, and improvisations mimetic with, or paralleling" (Berry, 1984, p. 151) the unique psychic expression.

From an archetypal perspective, the dream, in its presentation as such, has already produced a meaningful expression of the psyche—the dream is primary (Berry, 1984). Interpretation is a secondary activity that has the potential to render further meaning from the dream. From an archetypal perspective, the interpretive act can be most accurate and effective when it is done via mimesis of the values already expressed by the dream itself. As Berry noted:

> In an interpretation . . . [the manifest shape of the dream] must be re-rendered but in a way fitting to or made possible by the original—within the same tone or key, yet as a contrasting variation or improvisation of it.
>
> (p. 153)

Singular interpretations may facilitate a powerful insight, but they come with the heavy price of losing the natural fecundity of the image. An archetypal model for interpretation might note something from a particular perspective, but the formulation is held in mind as one perspective among many—seeing through what was said, to who was saying it, thus acknowledging the always-relative quality of any interpretation.

Berry's (1982) work has offered a clear depiction of the relativity of interpretation—offering those who work with dreams an opportunity to reflect on the various fantasies that, for better or worse, shape the interpretations made when encountering a dream. Turning the task of "interpretive self-awareness" on her own approach, she notes a fundamental assumption of archetypal psychotherapy: the dream is "an imaginal product in its own right. Despite what we do or don't do with it—it is an image" (p. 57).

As an image, each dream arrives with its own context, which is prior to even the most apparent analogy to waking life context. As Berry (1982) noted, the dream itself has texture, text, and weave. As the body of the image, its sensuality and place, becomes more differentiated through careful attention, the dream will begin to locate itself as situated within a particular psychic domain. For example, the dream noted above presents a variety of circumstances, which when taken together form a setting within which the dream may begin to be understood on its own terms. "Mother's house" and "father's car" set the "I" in the dream as a "son-I," a child of, parented by that which is present in the dream. Linking the dream to day world context would bind the images to the dreamer's literal family, placing a developmental lens over the dream, reshaping the presenting image within the fantasy of linear time and causal development. However, Berry (1982) has argued: "With imagination any question of objective referent is irrelevant. . . . As we read from Jung, images in our dreams are not reflections of external objects but are 'inner images"' (p. 57).

Jung (1928/1966) described reading the dream at the subjective level, differentiating his approach to the dream from Freud's reading of the dream on the objective level. An interpretation on the subjective level involves referring "every part of the dream and all the actors in it back to the dreamer himself" (p. 84). Importantly, this mode of interpretation was coupled with what Jung called the synthetic or constructive method. This interpretive stance involved reinforcing and extending meaning through the use of amplification. Jung wrote: "Just as analysis breaks down the symbolical fantasy-material into its components, so the synthetic procedure integrates it into a general and intelligible statement" (p. 81). These three levels of interpretation, objective, subjective, and synthetic, offer different pathways into the dream, each revealing and concealing the different meanings embedded in the dream motif.

Archetypal psychology stands apart from both Jung and Freud by sticking close to the investigation of what the psyche is saying about itself through the dream. Hillman (1979a), in his highly polemical style, has offered a strong critique of both objective and subjective methods. He wrote:

> Dare I say it loud and clear? The persons I engage with in dreams are neither representations (*simulacra*) of their living selves nor parts of myself. They are shadow images that fill

> archetypal roles; they are personae, masks, in the hollow of which is a *numen*.
>
> (pp. 60–61)

He added: "The dream image of a human person cannot be taken in terms of his actuality, since the image in a dream belongs to the underworld shades and therefore refers to an archetypal person in human shape" (p. 61).

It is essential to note that Hillman's vehement rhetoric is aimed at impressing upon the reader the ubiquitous tendency to move away from the dream into waking life and to reduce the dream to that which can be known and used by the ego. In reading Hillman, it is important to think critically about what he is saying and avoid the trap of literalizing his argument. For example, personal associations to a dream figure need not only elucidate the personal level of the dream image. The psyche has chosen to weave an image out of this particular figure: one's personal associations to that figure may help further qualify the appearance of this image, clarifying the archetypal constellation to which it belongs. Even Hillman (1979a) relents from his mission to de-humanize the dream, conceding to a both-and response to the question of personal vs. archetypal dimensions of the dream. He noted: "The persons with whom I had dinner and who return in my dream embody *both*, my traits and actions and divine traits and actions" (p. 100).

The interpersonal and intrapsychic dynamics depicted in a dream may be important focal points at certain times in one's work with a patient, however these positions can obscure archetypal dimensions of psychic phenomena. Hillman's (1979a) argument bespeaks the call, made by the psyche itself, to afford the widest sense of value to psychic image—to recognize that "in dreams we are visited by the daimones, nymphs, heroes, and gods shaped like our friends of last evening" (p. 62). The archetypal method is a process of reverting the image to its mythic origin, and as Hillman (1979a) has noted, "They become mythic beings, not mainly by amplifying their mythic parallels but by seeing through to the imaginative persons within the personal masks. Only the persons of the dream are essential for understanding the persons in the dream" (pp. 63–64).

To foster this archetypal dimension of the dream and stick to the presenting image, it might be useful to imagine that the dream is sealed off from waking life experience—all references and relationships are to other aspects of the image—as if the dream cared little for the dreamer's historical experience. Of course this approach will eventually drop away as analogies to waking life fill one's mind, however, this stance defends against the tenacious habit of tearing dreams from the context inherent to the image.

By sticking to the imaginal context of the dream, the father and mother of the dream noted above become de-literalized, qualified not by the dreamer's parents but by the images to which these roles appear. The "I" in the dream is also an image-I, contextualized by the dream. An archetypal approach to the dream fosters a perspective that can see the many "I"s of the psyche, allowing them autonomy distinct from the "I" that observes the dream. Hillman (1979a) noted: "Ego-behavior in the dream reflects the pattern of the image and the relations within the image, rather than the patterns and relations of the dayworld" (p. 102).

Keeping the "I" in the dream as a particular "I" contextualized by the dream itself maintains the already given-over weave of the image. The "interlocking" (Hillman, 1978, p. 157) of each element of the dream is further supported by highlighting the relationships between the images within the larger overall image of the dream itself. To elucidate the imaginal context and open up the metaphorical implication of each image, Hillman (1978) has made use of a style of notation, which he calls when-then, a method that links one image with another as contextually necessary. Berry (1982) referred to the essential importance of each image and the relationships between each image as the intra-relation, or "the full democracy of the image" (p. 60).

In the above example, the dream sets the "I" at the driveway of the mother's house, or perhaps this image depicts the drive toward mother, or the mother of the drive. The when-then notation highlights the following relationships: *When* the drive is occupied by the car of father, *then* it is viewed by the "I" from the rear. *When* the "I" sees from behind the father's car, that which he drove or that which drove him, *then* he feels anxious about instability, wants to get on more solid ground, is stuck in ambivalence.

As the metaphors inherent to the image become more apparent, the dream begins to pose particular questions:

> *Is the way I drive (my life, my work, my "looking at the rear-end") father to instability and the anxiety of groundlessness—the fear of toppling over? Or, do I father anxiety with my dug up way of driving towards "mother's house?" What would it be like to fall*

> *in the pit of my drives? Has my "mother-drive" gone underground where it threatens to swallow up my father's car (my ability to move, to separate from mother, to penetrate the world)? When I am on a drive towards the mother, then I see the car that drove my father as unstable, in danger of toppling into groundlessness. Is the solid matter of my drive towards mother de-stabilized and losing ground? How have I felt insecure about getting in father's car—taking his place, toppling over in the driver's seat?*

In addition to showing the intra-relatedness of the dream images, where "all parts have an equal right to be heard and belong to the body politic" (Berry, 1982, p. 60), following the context of the image with the when-then notation also demonstrates Berry's notion of the simultaneity of the image. In the above dream, all the features arrive together as one highly specified constellation.

The same quality of simultaneity is present in psychopathology. For example, the various symptoms of depression: sadness, irritability, loss of interest, psychomotor retardation—these features arrive together as a full gestalt. They are related but not by causation. In holding these differentiated pieces together as expressions of the particularity of the depression, one may understand the quality and feeling-tone of the individual's experience—the image of the depression. With both symptom and dream, we might imagine the sequence of presenting images as "a series of superimpositions, . . . each event adding texture and thickening to the rest" (p. 59).

Whereas each image always has belonging in the dream, some images stand out as holding more poetic value. Berry (1982) has argued that images that appear as striking in their peculiarity may be assumed "to be of high value because they are examples of the *opus contra naturam*" (p. 62). Like a symptom, they stand out from what is normal and to be expected. They call to be attended to, and take the mind outside of conventional (ego) expectations.

Peculiar images, like the car halfway suspended over an absent drive, invoke a sense of curiosity. They simultaneously protect the dream from simplistic reduction while also inviting the dreamer to marvel at the strange depiction—the value hidden in the repulsive and absurd, inciting/insighting in the individual the recognition that psychic phenomena, symptoms, feelings, fantasies, dreams, all have significance.

A dream may also open up by turning this idea upside-down, imagining the most usual, ordinary, and mundane image as laden with value. Banal experience, the tedium of the daily grind, when encountered as image, is given opportunity to show that it too has metaphorical import, psychic *gravitas*. A man goes to work all day and that night dreams that he is at his place of employment making copies for his fat boss. This scene, so easily dismissed upon waking, is undoubtedly packed with meaning. Affording value to this dream may offer an opportunity to recognize the way this man feels mechanized at work, just another copy, being swallowed by his boss's demands. Perhaps dreaming the mundane is the psyche's way of bringing depth to that which is easily dismissed as soulless, a recognition that all experiences are imbued with imaginal activity and metaphorical implication.

## Imaginal therapy

The adherence to metaphor and image has required archetypal psychologists to explicate a clinical method that places image as primary. As Hillman and Berry stated in an unpublished lecture: "Ours could be called an *image-focused therapy*. Thus the dream as an image or bundle of images is paradigmatic, as if we were placing the entire psychotherapeutic procedure within the context of a dream" (as cited in Hillman, 2004). With therapy as dream, the events that occur throughout the session are rooted in a metaphorical position—all phenomena throughout the hour become seeds for psychological reflection.

One method that is central to image-making is Hillman's (1975a, 1975b, 1979a) use of *epistrophe*, or reversion—a notion derived from Henry Corbin's (1997) description of *ta'wil*. Reversion involves placing a phenomenon in its archetypal context through following the links made by resemblance. Reversion, Hillman (1979a) wrote, is:

> a method which connects an event to its image, a psychic process to its myth, a suffering of the soul to the imaginal mystery expressed therein. Epistrophe, or the return through likeness, offers to psychological understanding a main avenue for recovering order from the confusion of psychic phenomena, other than Freud's idea of development and Jung's of opposites.
>
> (p. 4)

Whereas, Hillman has exercised reversion most often in relation to theory, this method has an essential place in archetypal praxis.

It takes little clinical experience to learn that the apparently simple task of sitting with an individual in a consulting room for 50 minutes can quickly start to feel terrifying as one attempts to navigate amidst the chaotic maelstrom of psychic content. This experience has led to the essential need for some sort of organizing filter. In the above passage, Hillman makes reference to both Freud's and Jung's primary filters—fantasies through which psychic phenomena may be perceived, organized, and narrated. The fantasy, whether it is developmental or compensatory, is a metaphor, and like all metaphors it both is and is not. The fantasy of reversion, while certainly not beyond criticism, opens phenomena to the multiplicity present in myth, thereby, it is hoped, avoiding reduction into a mechanized system of interpretation. In addition, reversion, as a hermeneutic position for the therapist and patient, encourages both parties to stick close to the particularity of the phenomena. As Hillman (1979a) noted, "only by scrutinizing the event at hand can we attempt to find which of many archetypal constellations it might resemble" (p. 4).

Importantly, the move is not from event to myth, rather, one locates the event in the cosmos of myth through resemblance, and then works with the weave of both as an image. Whereas this move certainly has its roots in Jungian analysis, archetypal psychology differentiates itself, as was argued above, by avoiding abstraction into symbolic interpretation.

Take, for example, the following unpublished account of Hillman (1975c) working with one of his own dreams:

> *Looking for an image, looking for a soul figure. I climb the tower into the keep. An empty room. No princess, no Sheila-Danielle any longer in the towering glans, this high, that is a pencil point, that exudes a continuous creamy semen.*

Hillman allows personal and archetypal associations to dance in and out of the page. They enter and then give way to the next analogy in an always-shifting flow of meaning. He offers them to the dream, and the dream accepts them and continues its going-on-being (Winnicott, 1971). He prevents the amplificatory references from impinging on the dream by returning quickly to the image. Analytic interpretations, on the other hand, tend to stop the flow, saying this is it. The image is taken apart,[4] and the meaning is deciphered.

Hillman (1975c) added: "*Descending into the grounds. An old man with clothbound feet, feet wrapped in felt, a vague figure, like the hooded man in the Michelagelo self-portrait. We walk in the grounds to and fro, two old men, caretakers, taking care.*" The dream text gains the richness of a cultural association to the Michelangelo self-portrait. It swells with more meaning and reference, becomes more voluminous. He plays with the language of the dream, noting the way in which the image of caretakers implies taking care. He goes on to explore the imagistic implications of "feet wrapped in felt." The "felt feet" in the garden is juxtaposed with the empty room at the height of the tower.

Hillman's mode of dream work is like a dance with the presenting image—a relational experience in which other images are made through the language of the dream, associations, and similarities. Hillman exemplifies a kind of active imagination within the dream text, preserving the psychic phenomena by sticking to the image while also engaging it actively through play.

### Image work

Throughout the literature of archetypal psychology, one finds continual reference to one of the primary axioms of archetypal practice: "stick to the image" (Berry, 1982; Hillman, 1975a, 1978, 1979b). This motto endorses a methodological stance that preserves the particular meaning presented in the always-unique image by vivifying the details of the image. As noted above, the archetypal practitioner avoids abstractions and interpretations that turn a living, dynamic, and precisely qualified image into a mere concept. Ontological priority is given to the image, affirming its position as "that to which we return again and again, and that which is the primary ground and spring of our imaginal awareness" (Berry, 1982, p. 64).

When working with a dream or fantasy, the practitioner has an opportunity to step into the world that the image presents, to operate with the language and epistemology native to that particular image, positioning him- or herself within the imaginal motif—language, gesture, style, perspective, interpretation, all born from the image. When amplification is employed, it is used in service to the specificity of the image not as a hermeneutic method of deciphering the hidden or latent meaning. Using an alchemical metaphor, the image is afforded a contained space in the rudiment of the psyche, repeatedly dissolved and coagulated, heated and cooled, dried and moistened, and through these operations, the image becomes like a tincture—a potent medicinal of psychic origin.

As the material is worked, the dream motif restated through a playful waterfall of language, punctuation is fluid or removed, words conjoined or hyphenated, compounds de-compounded, language is allowed its multiple meanings, the body of the dream fills out, "a thickening occurs" (Berry, 1984, p. 161), and the dream-to-life similarities emerge.

Hillman (1977) noted, "we can meet the soul in the image and understand it . . . through word play which is also a way of talking with the image and letting it talk. We watch its behavior—how the image behaves within itself" (p. 81). The primary material from which the play ensues is the constellation of language given over by the image. The words used to describe the image are the essential factor in the working of the dream as image—as Hillman (1978) noted: "There is nowhere else to look to find their significance" (p. 170). Berry (1982) described the linguistic play as a kind of "restatement," which discloses "a metaphorical nuance, echoing or reflecting the text beyond its literal statement" (p. 72). She added, "This might be done in two ways: first by replacing the actual word with synonyms and equivalents.. .. Second, by simply restating in the same words but emphasizing the metaphorical quality within the words themselves" (p. 72).

Take, for example, the following dream:

> *One of the guys who paints his face blue (the Blue Man Group) was showing my girlfriend and me how to apply white make up to our face, so it could be painted with color. I began applying the white make up. I was surprised by how quickly it began covering over the features of my face.*

When the guy who is blue in the face shows us how to make up, not down, my face goes white. When I make up, I cover my face (in shame?). He made a show of how to white-out my face, making up my features—teaching me how I lose face. Is he blue in the face telling me how to make up with my girlfriend?

When the "me" is shown, he is in conjunction with the "my girlfriend" who is also a "shown my girlfriend," a necessary pairing. Only when the "me" is with the "shown my girlfriend" does the "Man with the Blues," who is blue in the face, show. The dream precisely demarcates the constellation of a complex.

As the image has now revealed some of its inherent metaphors, it has also become a ripe field of analogy, connecting to a multitude of waking life phenomena and psychological patterns. Through a simple question inviting the dreamer to reflect on what this dream is like, the image is given opportunity to reach into the dreamer's life and make itself matter. For example:

> *The white face make up is like when I put on a face to cover over my embarrassment at a party, the whiteness of oblivion that I want to move into. It's like when I panic about someone not liking me, like dissociating when I have strong feelings. Its like making myself into a blank canvas—ready to accommodate the color I need to be, molding myself, disguising my 'true color' and the features that make me an individual. Going white is like blending in, not wanting to stand out—like facing the world with my white privilege.*

When a dreamer begins to connect the dream image to similar patterns, behaviors, feelings, fantasies, and memories, the wealth of links abound, the image begins to show its depth, and the dreamer is given an opportunity to experience the veracity and value of psychic reality. Unlike interpretation, analogy does not stop with a singular meaning. One analogy flows into another, filling out a complex constellation and constellating a complex. All this comes while sticking close to the precise portrayal of the image.

Hillman (1977) has noted the way in which archetypal psychotherapy employs analogy in a similar fashion as anatomists, where an analogical relationship implies "likeness in *function* but not in *origin*" (p. 86). Whereas implying origin is a move toward simplistic reduction, with analogy the relationship between a dream image and a mythological motif can be explored without implicitly or explicitly indicating that the image is of one or another archetype.

By working in terms of likenesses, the ambiguity of the image is maintained, which in turn gives rise to further fantasy—the dream continues to dream itself. Furthermore the web of similarity carried by each image discloses its place in the family of things, where and how the idiosyncratic and personal dimensions of the image belong within the cosmos of archetypal significance (Hillman, 1975d).

Another dream:

> *I am at my mother's house standing at the counter in the kitchen. As a birthday gift, my girlfriend gives me a black snake tightly bound in a package and seemingly lifeless. It had been tied*

> *together and appeared to be manufactured and mass-produced. I unwrap the snake and it begins to unfold and fill out. I read the package. The snake is supposed to be harmless. I go to the bathroom, intending to keep the snake contained there.*

When I am at my mother's house, countering, then my girlfriend gives. When girlfriend-in-mother's-house gives, then a black snake is tightly bound. Is there also a tightness and a boundedness between girlfriend and mother, packaging lifelessness? When the "I" that is at my mother's house is gifted by the girlfriend, then lifeless black snake is manufactured and produced in mass. When the my-girlfriend and the standing-in-mother's-house-I are tied together lifelessly, given is the unfolding and filling out of the black snake.

As the relationships of the image are disclosed, the image comes alive with highly qualified personifications like the standing-in-mother's-house-I. With a psychologically attuned ear, this may read simply as a mother complex, but the image says so much more than this conceptual abstraction. Watch the particularity that comes with sticking to the image. This I-mother-girlfriend relationship is countered in the kitchen, where it cooks, where it feeds, where the "I" takes a stand and counters mother-girlfriend—the constraining feminine that ties up the black snake, counters instinct.

Just as the black snake appeared lifeless and bound at first, only coming to life as it is unwrapped, when an image is afforded attention, it begins to unfold and fill out. As the dreamer of this dream, I am left not with dead words like repressed libido and maternal enmeshment. Rather, I am left to wonder about bound-black-snakeness and the bound up, lifeless quality in my relationship with my girlfriend and prior to that my mother. Is the snake really harmless or is this simply the wish of the ego-girlfriend complex—how the snake has been packaged? I am also left to wonder how I have been complicit in binding this snake. Have I projected it into my girlfriend, and she is giving it back to me on my birthday—a rebirthing of black-snakeness?

Extending the when-then notation further, Hillman (1978) has suggested the value of eternalizing the image by turning the *when* of the when-then sequence into *whenever*. For example, the sequence noted above: when harmlessness is supposed, the "going to the bathroom I" intends to keep the snake contained, shows a relationship between supposing harmlessness, a bathrooming I, and the intent to maintain containment of the snake. By eternalizing the relationship, the image is endowed with more value: Whenever harmlessness is supposed, the "going to the bathroom I" intends to keep the snake contained. The relationship becomes inextricable—each feature essential to this dynamic.

A similar effect may be developed through singularizing the image. By placing *only* in front of the *when*, the occasion in which the dream action occurred is specified (Hillman, 1978). In addition to further specifying the image, singularizing helps prevent the generalization of a psychological dynamic depicted in a dream. Hillman noted the despairing quality that can arrive when an image presents as dead, dying, or grotesque. When generalized, the dreamer can begin to feel as if their entire psychic life is reflected by the disturbing image. Singularizing the image makes the image stick to its relativized presentation.

Another technique noted by Hillman involves contrasting the presenting image with a different image. He considers this technique particularly useful when the dreamer indicates that he or she has no fantasy in relation to the image—no idea why this image in this dream. Holding one image against another encourages the dreamer to pick out a distinguishing element to the particular dream image and begins to give the image a sense of necessity.

Hillman (1978) has also noted the value of doing nothing to an image but simply allowing it to stay near. He refers to this as "keeping images" and indicates that it is particularly useful when an image feels hard, dense, impenetrable. As the image sits near, one may keep a peripheral eye on it and notice any changes, any sign of life that may emerge as time passes. Often the material that arrives spontaneously in the time of keeping images helps illuminate the matter of the image.

Lastly, Hillman (1977) advised those working with dreams to pay attention to the disjunctions in the dream, "the hiatus" (that is, *when, but, suddenly, then, until, however, later*). "The image now has an internal tension, the inklings of a plot, even a smoulder of anticipation" (p. 72). In an elaboration of this idea, he added: "When these occur in the midst of an image they announce a hiatus in the hidden connections which may be signifying a hidden disconnection, a juxtaposition that makes the spark of consciousness leap across empty space" (Hillman, 1978, p. 182).

### *Image sense*

Hillman (1979b) noted that the process of working with dreams invokes a shift from one's typical sense perception: the senses themselves become metaphors (or metamorphosed). One sees an image, but not through the retina of the eye. Rather the image is seen through imagination, which means we not only perceive its form but we also "see" the implications intrinsic to its form. We hear the narrative of the dream, but we also "hear" the metaphors constellated by the presenting images. As the image pulls the dreamer into imagination, the senses, so often the organ of literalism, become the *via regia*, deepening the image into its multiple meanings. As Hillman has noted, the word "sense" refers to both "concrete, physical, directly tangible, and also, meaning, significance, direction, invisibly mental" (p. 136). The senses make sense of the image, sensitizing the dreamer to the dream and facilitating sensitivity to the particularity of each image.

As such, the dream is entered by way of aesthetics. Here, Hillman is closely following Jung, "holding that the careful aesthetic elaboration of a psychic event is its meaning" (Hillman, 1979b, p. 135). This careful elaboration means holding to the image as such, complete, fulfilled, allowing imagination to speak the significance implied by the image itself. The move from manifest to latent no longer involves a move away from the derivative image toward the unrepresented singular dream-thought. Instead, the move into the latent meaning of the dream is evoked by carefully and repeatedly turning the image in one's mind, hearing its metaphors speak. Experientially, the image begins to take space in the dreamer's mind. The individual steps into the image and lives through it. As further events unfold, the image is analogically coupled with waking life, relationships, psychodynamics. As Hillman noted: "We can amplify an image from within itself, simply by attending to it more sensitively, tuning in, focusing" (p. 139). This is not to say that the knowledge drawn from amplificatory reference is no longer useful. One's knowledge of symbol, cultural reference, and psychological concepts all become useful in how one hears the image. As the image begins to take life, it evokes a gravitational pull in which mythological motif, personal associations, other dreams and fantasies, and similar therapeutic themes find a pattern of orbit, furthering the differentiation of the individual's psychic cosmology.

In addition, one may choose to temporarily color the image with a particular referent, as if one were staining a slide for use with a microscope. The stain helps enhance contrast and illuminate detail. Different stains will illuminate and differentiate the various components of the image. Importantly, the biologist, after applying a stain to a sample, would not then focus his or her attention on the stain itself. Similarly, in image-focused psychotherapy, the amplificatory or conceptual reference does not take precedence over the presenting image.

As Watkins (1984) noted, training as a psychologist provides an individual with a retinue of tools that may ultimately prove antithetical to one's work with the image. An idea, a concept, or a mythological amplification is only useful if it opens the image (Hillman, 1975a). Concepts, like symbols, most often pull one's attention away from the image to an established psychological formulation. Hillman (1975a) stated: "Though their image, behavior, and mood leads us to recognize them as 'anima' and 'father,' and though we even gain insight through this archetypal recognition, we do not literally see the anima or the father" (p. 144).

## Qualitative differentiation

The elaboration of events into images, whether in dream or waking life, is largely dependent on the particular way in which the nouns, the concrete persons, places, and things, are qualified by modifiers (Hillman, 1978). In working from an archetypal perspective, attending to these qualifiers becomes an essential part of the process. The practitioner links the modifiers to the nouns and relates to them as necessary to each other.

The idiosyncratic qualities within which an image appears, its context, mood, and scene, is what distinguishes an image from a symbol (Hillman, 1977). Whereas symbolic modes of interpretation offer the benefit of connecting the dream and thereby the dreamer with a larger collective reality, the always-qualified image illuminates the unique characteristics of the complex in its precise portrayal of *intra*-related features. The image differentiates the psychic event.

Hillman (1978) has described the way in which reversing the image through reversing the usual mode of speech, making nouns into descriptors, opens new perspectives in relation to the dream. He noted: "Not only can images be reversed; the act of reversing is a step in making images" (p. 164). For example, one of the dreams noted above featured a black snake. In reversing the language of the image, one could also imagine a snake-like blackness, a depiction of the way in which my blackness snakes along—out of sight and underground, coiled and bound.

This notion of the reversibility of the dream speech can also assist in making images of the verbs in the dream. Hillman (1978) noted: "A first step in imaging a verb is to keep it attached to an adverb" (p. 167). To continue with our example, the dream text reads: my girlfriend gives me a black snake tightly bound. In bringing the adverb and the verb together, we now have *gives tightly*. Reversing this we have tightly giving. An image has formed around the way in which the "my girlfriend" tightly gives. Or to reverse once more, when the dream ego receives, tightness is a given. Hillman has suggested that the verb-image can differentiate specific mechanisms used by the dreamer, for example, the way I go tight when my girlfriend gives me my blackness.

## Caveat

It is important to note that the development of the metaphorical sensibility on which archetypal psychotherapy is dependent, is in fact a significant psychological accomplishment. Individuals functioning at a borderline or psychotic level of organization often relate to their psychological experience as a thing-in-itself. This has been described by psychoanalytic authors, such as Hanna Segal (1957), as symbolic equation, and has come to be associated with profoundly difficult psychotherapeutic treatments. It is this author's opinion that archetypal psychotherapy is not the primary treatment of choice in such instances. Working with individuals organized at a borderline or psychotic level may require years of careful work in the transference field before they are able to play with psychic images.

## Notes

1 The terms *clearing* and *horizon* have been used by phenomenologists like Heidegger and Gadamer to describe one's situatedness in a cultural context. Cultural artifacts like language and the various other social practices shape what is available to perception—the clearing through which one experiences the world. The image of the forest clearing was a metaphor often used by Heidegger to describe unconcealment.

2 Here conclusion can mean both "a compendious or inclusive statement or description," or "a problem, riddle, enigma" (Conclusion, 2008).

3 Philemon was an imaginal figure that appeared often in Jung's active imagination experiments. The relationship between Jung and Philemon is most directly represented in the recently published *Red Book* (Jung & Shamdasani, 2009).

4 Analysis: "The breaking down of a substance into simpler constituents" (Analysis, 2008).

## References


Analysis. (2008). In *Oxford English dictionary online* (3rd ed.). Retrieved from www.oed.com.pgi.idm.oclc.org/view/Entry/38312?redirectedFrom=analysis#eid

Berry, P. (1982). *Echo's subtle body: Contributions to an archetypal psychology.* Putnam, CT: Spring.

Berry, P. (1984). Jung's early psychiatric writing: The emergence of a psychopoetics (Unpublished Doctoral Dissertation). University of Dallas, Dallas, TX.

Casey, E. S. (1974). Toward a phenomenology of imagination. *The Journal of the British Society for Phenomenology*, *5*(10), 29–52.

Conclusion. (2008). In *Oxford English dictionary online* (3rd ed.). Retrieved from www.oed.com.pgi.idm.oclc.org/view/Entry/38312?redirectedFrom=conclusion#eid

Corbin, H. (1997). *Alone with the alone: Creative imagination in the Sūfism of Ibn Árabī* (R. Manheim, Trans.). Princeton, NJ: Princeton University Press.

Freud, S. (1953). *The Interpretation of dreams: The complete and definitive text* (J. Strachey & G. Zilboorg, Trans.). New York, NY: Basic Books. (Original work published 1900)

Freud, S. (1964). *New introductory lectures on psycho-analysis.* (W. J. H. Sprott, Trans.). New York, NY: W. W. Norton. (Original work published 1933)

Freud, S. (1975). *Beyond the pleasure principle.* (J. Strachey & G. Zilboorg, Trans.). New York, NY: Norton. (Original work published 1920)

Hillman, J. (1972). *The myth of analysis.* Evanston: Northwestern University Press.

Hillman, J. (1975a). *Re-visioning psychology.* New York, NY: Harper and Row.

Hillman, J. (1975b). *Loose ends: Primary papers in archetypal psychology.* Putnam, CT: Spring.

Hillman, J. (1975c). Modes of thought. [Unpublished notes]. The James Hillman Collection (A75b, 2.26). OPUS Archives and Research Center, Carpinteria, CA.

Hillman, J. (1975d). Modes of thought. [Unpublished notes]. The James Hillman Collection (A75b, 108). OPUS Archives and Research Center, Carpinteria, CA.

Hillman, J. (1977). An inquiry into image. *Spring*, *44*, 62–88.

Hillman, J. (1978). Further notes on images. *Spring*, *45*, 152–182.

Hillman, J. (1979a). *Dream and underworld.* New York, NY: Harper and Row.

Hillman, J. (1979b). Image-sense. *Spring*, *46*, 130–143.

Hillman, J. (2004). *Archetypal psychology.* Putnam, CT: Spring.

Jung, C. G. (1965). *Memories, dreams, reflections.* New York, NY: Vintage Books.

Jung, C. G. (1971). Psychological types. In H. Read, M. Fordham, G. Adler, & W. McGuire (Eds.), *The collected works of C. G. Jung* (R. F. C. Hull, Trans.) (Vol. 6). Princeton, NJ: Princeton University Press. (Original work published 1921)

Jung, C. G. (1954a). Foreword to Suzuki's introduction to Zen Buddhism. In H. Read, M. Fordham, G. Adler, & W. McGuire (Eds.), *The collected works of C. G. Jung* (R. F. C. Hull, Trans.) (Vol. 11, pp. 538–557). Princeton, NJ: Princeton University Press. (Original work published 1939)

Jung, C. G. (1954b). Psychological commentary on the Tibetan book of the great liberation. In H. Read, M. Fordham, G. Adler, & W. McGuire (Eds.), *The collected works of C. G. Jung* (R. F. C. Hull, Trans.) (Vol. 11, pp. 475–508). Princeton, NJ: Princeton University Press. (Original work published 1939)

Jung, C. G. (1959). Conscious, unconscious, and individuation. In H. Read, M. Fordham, G. Adler, & W. McGuire (Eds.), *The collected works of C. G. Jung* (R.

F. C. Hull, Trans.) (Vol. 9i, pp. 151–275). Princeton, NJ: Princeton University Press. (Original work published 1939)

Jung, C. G. (1960). The real and the surreal. In H. Read, M. Fordham, G. Adler, & W. McGuire (Eds.), *The collected works of C. G. Jung* (R. F. C. Hull, Trans.) (Vol. 8, pp. 382–384). Princeton, NJ: Princeton University Press. (Original work published 1933)

Jung, C. G. (1966). The relations between the ego and the unconscious. In H. Read, M. Fordham, G. Adler, & W. McGuire (Eds.), *The collected works of C. G. Jung* (R. F. C. Hull, Trans.) (2nd ed., Vol. 7, pp. 123–244). Princeton, NJ: Princeton University Press. (Original work published 1928)

Jung, C. G., & Shamdasani, S. (2009). *Liber novus*. New York, NY: W.W. Norton & Co.

Obama, B. H. (2012, July 13). Remarks by the president at a campaign event in Roanoke, Virginia. Retrieved from www.whitehouse.gov/the-press-office/2012/07/13/remarks-president-campaign-event-roanoke-virginia

PDM Task Force. (2006). *Psychodynamic diagnostic manual*. Silver Spring, MD: Alliance of Psychoanalytic Organizations.

Schenk, R. (1989). The soul of beauty: A psychological investigation of appearance (Unpublished Doctoral Dissertation). University of Dallas, Dallas, TX.

Segal, H. (1957). Notes on symbol formation. *International Journal of Psychoanalysis*, *38*, 391–398.

Stolorow, R. D., Brandchaft, B., & Atwood, G. E. (1987). Psychoanalytic treatment: An intersubjective approach. Hillsdale, NJ: Analytic Press.

Watkins, M. (1984). *Waking dreams*. Dallas, TX: Spring.

Watkins, M. (1986). *Invisible guests: The development of imaginal dialogues*. Dallas, TX: Spring.

Winnicott, D. W. (1971). *Playing and reality*. New York, NY: Basic Books.

Chapter 3

# Archetypal psychodynamics

> Myths do not tell us how, they simply give us the invisible background which starts us imagining, questioning, going deeper.
>
> (Hillman, 1975a, p. 158)

One of the principle aims of archetypal theory is to uncover the guiding fantasies that shape how psychology approaches the psyche. These fantasies, it has been argued (Hillman, 1972, 1975a), are always archetypally determined—collective in their nature. As enactments of the collective unconscious, they find their root, their *archai*, in mythological motif. Depth psychological theory has always been subject to a particular myth that frames and guides the therapeutic interaction. As a guiding metaphor, the myth of therapy both reveals and conceals. The myth funnels the chaotic barrage of clinical content, offers both a way to see through and principles with which one can see, shapes what is attended to, and in turn what is presented.

Freud's use of the Oedipus myth marks psychology's discovery of the psyche's mythological underpinnings. Freud's experience of this story as a living reality allowed him to provide a wealth of insight into particular psychic phenomena that are archetypal in nature, namely competition, jealousy, triangulation, tragic loss, incestuous longing, and mourning. Freud's great move was to see that what we experienced as children, a powerful love for our mother and an equally powerful hatred for anyone who took her away, comes to form the basis for all other relationships, and psychic conflicts experienced as a child will continue to re-capitulate through symptomatic expression until they are effectively worked through. This insight was foundational in shaping Freud's (1916/1977) understanding of his metapsychology and therapeutic approach—ontogeny recapitulates phylogeny.

His psychoanalytic method eventually came to center on tracking these mercurial moments of early development through careful observation of the transference.

Since Freud's (1895/2004) first use of the term, transference has remained a primary focus in Freudian analysis and has come to occupy a more dominant role in contemporary derivatives of Jungian analysis. In the following section I will review some of the major perspectives on the concept of transference in hopes of providing the background necessary to differentiate an archetypal perspective.

## Evolution of the concept of transference

### *Freud's contribution to the notion of transference*

Freud (1912/1981) described the dynamics of neurosis as an introversion of libido—a state in which libido has withdrawn from the external world, influencing the psychological functioning of the individual through unconscious phantasy. He argued that the increase in unconscious libido activates "the subject's infantile imagos" (p. 5), which then influence the individual's perception of reality in a variety of ways.

Freud (1912/1981) noted that the impetus for this introversion of libido stems from the inevitable childhood experiences in which libidinal satisfaction was frustrated—the Oedipal conflict. In light of this frustration, one could see that it was, at that time, prudent to pull back from the external world where "the attraction of reality had diminished" (p. 6). Holding to the tenet that nature is fundamentally conservative, Freud believed that libido tends to regress and repeat the previous patterns—the dynamics of which would be shaped by the Oedipal trauma (Singer, 1970). Thus the transference would consist primarily of erotic feelings and phantasies, the aggressive impulse to attain and maintain the object's affection, and the anxieties associated with fantasies of transgressing a fundamental taboo.

In order to free the trapped libido, Freud believed that the analyst must overcome the resistances that the patient unconsciously constructed as means of protection and conservation of the symptom. According to Freud (1912/1981), when the investigation comes close to the unconscious portion of the complexes a certain ambivalent tension will arise in which the patient is divided between serving the resistances and proceeding with the analytical investigation. From this tension, and in satisfaction to the resistance, the unconscious material that surfaces will be transferred onto the analyst.

Freud's theory makes a clear differentiation between positive transference and negative transference. In regards to the positive transference, Freud (1912/1981) considered all of the conscious expressions of positive relations toward the analyst such as "sympathy, friendship, trust, and the like" (p. 7), to be softened expressions derived from a primal and unconscious sexual aim. Freud (1912/1981) wrote: "Originally we knew only sexual objects; and psychoanalysis shows us that people who in our real life are merely admired or respected may still be sexual objects for our unconscious" (p. 7). Freud's belief was that it is essential to remove both the negative transference as well as the erotic transference like a surgeon removes a tumor. He concluded that the transference would then serve the analysis admirably (Wolstein, 1954, p. 70).

Despite his admonishment that the negative and erotic transference must be removed and his statement that the transference is "*the most powerful resistance* to the treatment" (Freud, 1912/1981, p. 5), he stated unequivocally that the analysis of the transference was the heart of the analytic treatment.

> It is precisely they [the transference] that do us the inestimable service of making the patient's hidden and forgotten erotic impulses immediate and manifest. For when all is said and done, it is impossible to destroy anyone *in absentia* or *in effigie*.
>
> (p. 8)

### *Klein and Bion's contribution to the notion of transference*

Melanie Klein's contribution to the notion of transference expanded the theory to include several important additional factors. One of the primary additions was the consideration of the pre-oedipal roots of the transference, that is, the narcissistic transference. Klein postulated that object relationships exist from birth, and as Segal (1983) affirmed: "It is the understanding of the functioning of primitive phantasy that is the basis on which her understanding of the transference and its unconscious roots is based" (p. 269). In regards to primitive phantasy, Klein followed Freud's (1916/1977) statement that "primal fantasies are a phylogenetic endowment" (p. 461). Her therapeutic method is based largely on the assumption that pre-oedipal phantasy material is endogenous and collective in nature. She also followed Freud's assumption that phantasy has an integral relationship with the instincts. Segal (1964) noted: "Phantasy may be considered the psychic representative or the mental correlate, the mental expression of instincts" (p. 12).

A second expansion advocated by Klein (1952/1981) is the notion that the transference includes both elements from past relationships as well as aspects of the patient's current mental world. According to Klein, the admixture of past and current psychological material is projected *into* the analyst who then takes on the role of both good and bad objects. Wilfred Bion (1962), a Kleinian trained analyst, demonstrated the way in which projecting undigested psychological material, beta elements, into the therapist is actually a form of primal communication. Analysis of the transference from a Kleinian standpoint is a reworking of this unprocessed material into what Bion called alpha elements, which can then be digested and integrated by the patient. This shift from distant observation to an intimate dyadic relationship is one of the major contributions of Klein and Bion (Mitchell & Black, 1995).

A third element found in the work of Klein is that transference can be observed not just in direct statements regarding the analyst, but also in more subtle and indirect communications. In fact, Klein (1952/1981) surmised that the unconscious elements of the transference material can be found in the totality of material presented. For example, displacement of transference feelings can be found in discussion of the patient's intimate relationships, activities, work, and dreams. Klein concluded that this displacement often originates from a splitting defense in which the patient is attempting to preserve the good analyst by transferring the difficult feelings arising in the immediate analytical situation onto other people (Mitchell & Black, 1995).

A final important note regarding the Kleinian approach to the transference is that Kleinian analysts will often begin to work with the transference material from the very beginning of treatment. The fundamental idea backing this method is that the analyst should be willing to go right to the heart of the most anxiety provoking material in a way that empathically acknowledges the experience and makes room for it within the analytical relationship. This move, according to the Kleinians, provides the patient with a feeling of relief and an inclination to express difficult psychological material.

## ***Object relations and Jung's complex psychology***

Klein's theory of an internal object world shares several important features with Jung's psychology. Of particular note is the similarity with Jung's formulation of the relationship between instinct/archetype and fantasy image. As noted in Chapter 2, Jung (1933/1960) asserted: "We may say that the image represents the meaning of the instinct" (p. 204). As Andrew Samuels (1985) noted: "Jung wrote of unconscious fantasies as 'fantasies which "want" to become conscious' and which manifest in the form of images. . . . The unconscious fantasy derived from instinct *searches* for external objects with which, in Bion's word, to 'mate' " (p. 43). Jung's description of the dynamic interplay between fantasy images and external objects corroborates precisely with Klein's notion of projective identification.

A second important parallel is found in the emphasis on personified figures of the psyche. Foundational to Klein's theory and the larger school of object relations is the notion that the psyche is populated with a multitude of figures that have autonomy distinct from the will of the ego. These figures, called internal objects, have formed, according to Thomas Ogden (1983), through a defensive process involving "a splitting of the ego into parts that when repressed constitute internal objects which stand in a particular unconscious relationship to one another" (p. 227). Ogden also noted:

> This internal relationship is shaped by the nature of the original object relationship, but does not by any means bear a one-to one correspondence with it. . . . The internal object relationship may be later re-externalized by means of projection and projective identification in an interpersonal setting thus generating the transference and countertransference phenomena of analysis and all other interpersonal interactions.
>
> (p. 227)

In a seminal essay Jung (1934/1960) posed the following definition of a complex:

> the *image* of a certain psychic situation which is strongly accentuated emotionally and is, moreover, incompatible with the habitual attitude of consciousness. This image has . . . a relatively high degree of autonomy, so that it is subject to the control of the

> conscious mind to only a limited extent, and therefore behaves like an animated foreign body in the sphere of consciousness.
> (p. 96)

He then added, "the etiology of their origin is frequently a so-called trauma, an emotional shock or some such thing, that *splits off a bit of the psyche* [emphasis added]" (p. 98). Although asserting an environmental etiology, Jung postulated that the complexes are organized by archetypal dominants of the psyche.

Despite the historical schism between Jungian and Freudian schools of psychoanalysis, it has been noted (Samuels, 1985) that both Freud and Klein come close to establishing something quite similar to Jung's notion of an archetypal layer of the psyche in their postulation that primitive phantasy is endowed phylogenetically and is shaped by pre-subjective schemas.

The tension between early environment and innate disposition has been and remains a matter of emphasis in both Jungian and Freudian derivatives of psychoanalysis (Samuels, 1985). Where the emphasis lands is, to a certain extent, dependent on the idiosyncratic preference of the individual practitioner as well as the particular school with which one identifies.

Some theorists, such as Storr (as cited in Samuels, 1985) have attempted to simplify the distinction by postulating that an object relations approach would focus largely on the developmental origins of the dominant internal objects, and those following the work of Jung, would emphasize the inborn predispositions. However, such a clean generalization does not match the spectrum found among the clinicians of these schools. Samuels (1985) noted: "both Kleinians and the Developmental school of post-Jungians postulate an interaction [between environment and inborn predisposition]" (p. 43). Nevertheless, as a general heuristic, it may be assumed that an archetypal psychotherapist would likely argue that preexisting structures take ontological and therapeutic precedence over personal experience (Samuels, 1985; Hillman, 1975a).

In an attempt to differentiate internal objects from archetypal dominants, Samuels (1985) has argued that "whilst internal objects must have an archetypal component, they also derive from the external world and hence they are not *structures,* nor do they have the predisposing power of the archetype or innate pattern" (pp. 42–43). Jung (1934/1960) afforded the complex significant ontological status, postulating a direct connection between the complex and that which has been called the *numinosum*. He noted, "where the realm of complexes begins the freedom of the ego comes to an end, for complexes are psychic agencies whose deepest nature is still unfathomed" (p. 104).

As noted in Chapter 4, archetypal psychology has argued strongly for this distinction between archetypal image and internalized object, as exemplified by Berry's (1982) statement "with imagination any question of objective referent is irrelevant" (p. 57). The emphatic emphasis on the transubjective aspect of the image found in the literature of archetypal psychology should be read as a response to what Hillman (1975a) has called an excessive emphasis on subjectivity (p. 189). The point of his strong stand against reducing the imaginal to the personal stems from his adherence to Corbin's statement:

> In *ta' wil* one must carry sensible forms back to imaginative forms and then rise to still higher meanings; to proceed in the opposite direction (to carry imaginative forms back to sensible forms . . .) is to destroy the virtualities of the imagination.
>
> (Corbin, 1997, p. 240)

Jung was less dismissive of the personal factor. Samuels (1985) has noted the way in which Jung's notion of the complex serves as a bridge between the personal experience of the individual and the archetypal layer of the psyche: "Outer experiences in infancy and throughout life cluster round an archetypal core. Events in childhood, and particularly internal conflicts, provide this personal aspect" (p. 47). Jung (1934/1960) has argued that the individual moves in and out of states of projection and identification with the various complexes. As such the complexes will show up in therapy most directly via the transference field.

### Kohut's contribution to the notion of transference

The next big development in the psychoanalytic theory of transference came out of Heinz Kohut's (1971) self psychology. With the positing of a separate narcissistic line of development distinct from object relations, Kohut shifted the focus from the classical view of transferring material onto a separate object to the notion of a selfobject transference in which the patient is living in an unconscious merger with the object. In accounting for this distinction, the analyst is confronted with the task of differentiating the selfobject dimension and the object relations dimension of the transference material. In working with a selfobject transference, the analyst works to maintain an astute awareness regarding the particular need he or she is being asked to fulfill through the narcissistic merger. Kohut postulated that the psychological interplay with the analyst as a selfobject fills in the patient's deficits and allows the patient's nuclear self to become more integrated and independent.

The self psychologists classify the transference as the "patient's here-and-now experience of the analyst" rather than a distortion of the present in the effort to repeat past patterns (Mitchell & Black, 1995, p. 166). This move, which marks a dramatic shift from classical theory, implies that the patient's transference material is a subjectively valid experience of the analyst (p. 166). The intersubjectival school expanded this idea into the theory that the transference is a creation of both analyst and patient, emphasizing the "fully contextual interaction of subjectivities with reciprocal, mutual influence" (Mitchell & Black, 1995, p. 167).

### *Jung's contribution to the notion of transference*

Jung differentiated between personal and archetypal aspects of the transference, placing a significant emphasis on the latter. Samuels (1985) has suggested that Jung was concerned with preserving his distinct contribution to psychoanalysis, the collective unconscious, and thus limited his focus on the personal aspect of the transference. Jung's (1946/1966) major work on the phenomenology of transference was focused on expanding the notion from the personal to the transpersonal, arguing that the dynamics of therapy could not be reduced to the early development of the patient. For a full understanding of the therapeutic interchange, he argued, the transference dynamics must be brought into relation with mythic narrative.

His move away from the personal aspects of the transference was part of a larger initiative. Instead of using the transference to intensify the relationship between patient and analyst, thus making central the psychic conflicts that emerge between the two people present, Jung seemed to be more interested in analyst and patient turning their full attention toward direct experience of the patient's fantasy and dream images. A significant portion of the analyst's work, described by Jung (1934/1966) as an educative and synthetic approach, was to provide amplificatory material and guidance as the patient deepens his or her relationship with the presenting images.

Jung's perspective on the transference was quite different from Freud. Whereas Freud treated transference phenomena as a return of the repressed, a recapitulation of early developmental trauma, Jung imagined transference through a prospective fantasy. The patient puts into the analyst material that remains outside his or her conscious awareness in order to foster a meaningful relationship with the as yet unknown psychic content (Wiener, 2010). In this sense Jung's perspective has striking similarity to Bion's (1962) notion of normal, that is, communicative, projective identification.

Jung relied heavily on the alchemical metaphor to elucidate the various stages the patient would experience vis-à-vis the psyche of the analyst and his or her own psychic material. In *The Psychology of the Transference*, Jung (1946/1966) used ten of the images of the *Rosarium Philosophorum*, an alchemical text dating from 1550 CE, to describe the gradual differentiation and integration of the psychic opposites, the *coniunctio*, imaged in the *Rosarium* as the sexual union of the masculine *Sol* and the feminine *Luna*. Whereas a review of these enigmatic and complex images is beyond the scope of this study, it is important to take note of the underlying approach Jung used in his study of the transference.

It could be argued that Jung's psychological study of alchemy was a radical move away from the dominant structuralist mode that attempts to posit authoritative conceptual systems. His respect for the unknowable and mercurial depths of the psyche required a dialectic parallel that was equally non-conceptual and poetic. In alchemy, he found a tradition that required a metaphoric sensibility—a tradition rich in its exposition of symbolic content, qualitative differentiation, and respect for the unknown and unknowable. Exemplifying his profound respect for the enigmatic, Jung (1946/1966) used the following lines for his epigraph to *The Psychology of the Transference*: "I inquire, I do not assert; I do not here determine anything with final assurance; I conjecture, try, compare, attempt, ask" (p. 1).

Importantly, this move towards the mythopoetic as mirror for the processes of the psyche became a foundational method for archetypal psychology. Hillman (2004) asserted "by relying on myths as its primary rhetoric, archetypal psychology grounds itself in a fantasy that cannot be taken historically, physically, literally" (p. 31). Essential to this move is the word *myths*. An archetypal psychology requires a plurality of metaphor to match the polycentric nature of the psyche itself.

### *Hillman's contribution to the notion of transference*

Hillman (1975b, 2004, 2007) has argued that the singular focus on the hero-centric myth of Oedipus exemplified by some schools of psychoanalysis has induced a self-inflicted blindness similar to Oedipus himself. The rigid adherence to Oedipal dynamics as *the fundament* has repressed the natural polyphony of story within which the psyche flourishes. Following both Freud and Jung, Hillman (1972) has attempted to enrich the way in which psychologists approach, and thereby shape, the therapeutic encounter by offering a different story as guide for the enigmatic unfolding of psyche both in therapy and life.

Specifically, Hillman has re-visioned the notion of transference by locating these phenomena, so central to depth psychotherapy, within the dynamics of Apuleius's tale of Eros and Psyche. One primary implication stemming from this move is the positioning of the relational pattern of Eros, the creative/destructive embodiment of love, and Psyche, the beautiful mortal struggling through her initiatory process, as the governing narrative for the myriad transference phenomena that occur anytime two people share psychological intimacy. As a myth of initiation, this tale gives therapy a motif of psychic redemption through love, "yet," Hillman (1972) noted, "it does not leave out torture, suicide, and Hades" (p. 60).

Redemption, or the successful movement of psyche in and through the mythological motif, is a feature that is missing in both the Oedipus myth as well as Jung's favored mytheme of the hero's journey:

> An Oedipus complex, like the Oedipus tragedy, has no apparent redemption, nor does the hero of the night-sea-journey, who, becoming *senex*-king, must in the end himself be overthrown. The curse on the hero-king must pass to the next generations, and a psyche mimetic of these archetypal models will be locked in the blind and dark heroic struggle of the family problem.
>
> (Hillman, 1972, p. 60)

Alternatively, the Eros-Psyche motif ends with the redemption of the highest *coniunctio*: Psyche and Eros are joined together in the celebrating presence of the Gods. Hillman (1972) has argued that this union placed amidst the presence of the archetypal figures is a confirmation of an *a priori* feature of the tale: "The processes—today called psychodynamic—which we are forced to go through are mythically governed. What transpires *in* our psyche is not *of* our psyche; both love and soul finally and from the beginning belong to the realm of archetypal reality" (p. 104).

The patterns in which soul is made are archetypally determined. Anima, the soul-potential of each individual, "becomes psyche through love" and it is "eros which engenders psyche" (Hillman, 1972, p. 54). Eros acts as a medium, a metaxy or psychopomp, inducting one into, or binding one with, a particular, archetypally constituted, element of soul—like a mother to a child, or the nearly tangible link between two lovers. The *fascinosum* of the love relationship owes its power to the Daemonic force of Eros. The arrow of Eros binds the two together and fosters the container from which soul may take shape and grow. Love illumines Psyche, brings her out of dullness and opacity, leads her into the challenges that set her in the world where she connects to the opus of soul-making and the *mysterium* of archetypal initiation.

The Eros-Psyche myth describes the way soul-making takes place in the intermediary space formed by the erotic tension of relationship. However, this is a different tension than that which is found in Aphroditic love, where tension moves quickly to action and generativity (Hillman, 1972). Alternatively, Eros makes soul when the tension between action and inhibition can be maintained, bringing the instinctual impulses into a psychic container where they can be worked on and differentiated. The fruit of this tension is imagination.

One of the primary tasks of depth psychotherapy is to strengthen the propensity for holding instinctual-archetypal elements within the vessel of the therapeutic relationship, where the type of action engaged is primarily imaginative action, that is, in and through fantasy. Abstaining from the literal heats the material and fuels the longing that drives the soul. Like Psyche sorting seeds, the patient endures the burden of combing through an overwhelming pile of life events, reliving the emotional experiences through the transference. Inhibitions that prevent the emergence of affect and action that would quickly eclipse the burgeoning psychic space become primary points of reflection, thus strengthening the patient's imaginative capacity.

As Psyche held the tension between utter despair and her passionate longing for Eros, she was given critical assistance without which she would be lost. Importantly, the source of the help came not from a hero figure, but from little creatures, the ants, and from the hawk, and an un-named river god. In a similar fashion, perhaps the resolution of the transference has less to do with heroic interpretations from the therapist and more to do with the timely emergence of guidance from those non-human figures occupying the space between therapist and patient. The tale suggests that the archetypal images appearing in dream and fantasy are the *via regia* toward cure, and the work of the therapist is to witness the struggle and to experience with the patient the intensity and vicissitudes inherent to the making of soul.

Imagining transference as an archetypal phenomenon places the therapeutic relationship within a transpersonal narrative. Viewed through the lens of Eros and Psyche, transference becomes not only a projection of "feelings, desires, and modes of relating formerly organized or experienced in connection with persons in the subject's past whom the subject was highly invested in" (Denis, 2005, p. 1776) but also a living out and through the mythological basis by which the psyche is shaped. As Hillman (1972) noted, "through the analyst the intentions of the *coniunctio* myth are transferred upon the analysand" (p. 109). Far from the blank screen of classical psychoanalysis, the archetypal therapist is imagined as a conduit for the initiation of Psyche into Eros and Eros into Psyche, experienced both between the people of the therapeutic relationship as well as the people of the psyche—the mythic figures that create through their qualities and interrelations what we have come to call psychodynamics.

As Samuels (1985) noted, Hillman's focus on mythic amplification of the transference situation positions him in close proximity to the classical Jungian approach to transference. However, if we follow out the implications of Hillman's work on image, we find an approach to the transference that is far more similar to contemporary psychoanalysis and the developmental school of analytical psychology.

The image of analysis and in analysis is the transference. Close work in the transference is a phenomenological engagement with the image—a two person active imagination (*cf.* Davidson, 1966). Contrary to Hillman's (1989) reductive critique of the psychoanalytic approach to transference, in which he argued "transference habitually deflects object libido, that is, love for anything beside analysis, into a narcissistic reflection upon analysis" (p. 65), transference work is not necessarily a reductive process. The therapist takes on a multitude of images and works alongside the patient to differentiate and experience their emotional presence. Transference is the way the therapist lends body to image. The image incarnates in her flesh, the sound of her voice, the paintings on her wall—the entire analytic setting is an imaginal topography. The frame surrounds the image.

The aim of directing primary focus to the transference in psychoanalytic practice is the same aim as the focus archetypal psychology affords image—to psychologize one's life, to see through literalism. Transference is the style in which the patient's life has been literalized—the reason why the patient is in therapy. Hillman's preference for "befriending" the image is expressing the same general approach psychoanalytic practitioners variously describe as "maternal reverie" (Bion, 1962, p. 309) "establishing a containing object" (Mitrani, 2001, p. 1085) and "taking the transference" (Mitrani, 1999, p. 47). Hillman describes befriending as a participation in the dream—"to enter into its imagery and mood, to want to know more about it, to understand, play with, live with, carry, and become familiar with" (p. 57). Although Mitrani (1999) pushes the idea further, arguing that "the analyst is able to feel herself to be that unwanted part of the patient's self or that unbearable object that had formerly been introjectively identified with by the patient" (p. 48), the parallels between an archetypal approach to image and a Bionian approach to transference are significant, calling into question Hillman's (1989) polemical stance against the emphasis psychoanalysis affords to working in the transference.

### *Phenomenology's contribution to the notion of transference*

Van den Berg (1972) wrote of the distinction between the abstract, unemotional world of scientific observation and the pre-reflective perceptions common to every human's lived experience. He argued that objects, contrary to the presumption of Cartesian-based natural science, do not exist apart from subjective experience; subject and object are co-created and shaped by the context within which they meet. Van den Berg wrote: "Never do we see objects without anything else. We see things within their context and in connection with ourselves: a unity which can be broken only to the detriment of the parts" (p. 37).

Carrying this argument further, Van den Berg (1961) has offered an important critique of the theory of projection and the conditions that made this theory necessary. Van den Berg tracked the historical emergence of the inner self, using one of Martin Luther's most influential essays, written in 1520, and Da Vinci's *Mona Lisa* as distinguishing moments in the development of an interior identity as separate and distinct from the external world. These cultural artifacts marked the moment when the human element became confined by the boundaries of skin. Subject and object were split and the notion of projection eventually became necessary as a link between the object and elements of one's interior identity. Van den Berg (1961) wrote: "The world is not contaminated with anything human; it may *seem* to be contaminated with it, but the theory of projection shows up the true nature of the contaminations: they are misplaced sentiments" (p. 217).

According to Van den Berg (1972), the phenomenon referred to as projection assumes that there are pure objects that reside outside the field of perception, and the patient, because of a mental illness, projects a "defective state of mind toward the objects he perceives" (p. 19). Van den Berg throws out the premise of pure objects, Descartes *res extensa*, and insists that so-called projections are in fact an accurate description of the patient's world. It is through taking the patient's observations seriously that the psychologist can begin to envision the lived experience of the suffering individual: "When the psychiatric patient tells what his world looks like, he states, without detours and without mistakes, what he is like" (p. 46). The world, according to phenomenologists, is always already imbued with subjectivity, which is given over to the individual. The depth psychological notion of an interiorized subjectivity that projects onto a disembodied world is a relic of the Cartesian split, and, as Van den Berg has demonstrated, does not accord with the lived experience of the individual.

In a move away from this lingering Cartesian ghost, phenomenology advocates for a therapeutic stance that takes seriously the lived reality of the individual, supplanting theory with description, and allowing the pre-reflective experience of the individual to speak for itself. The phenomenological psychologist avoids abstracting into obscure theoretical observations, and instead weaves a story based on "the interpretation of what he observes: hears, sees, smells, and feels" (Van den Berg, 1972, p. 77).

Following Van den Berg, Romanyshyn (2011) has brought this phenomenological critique more directly into the consulting room, arguing that transference is not a transfer of the patient's archaic objects onto the analyst, but rather it is an embodied enactment between two people. To carry out this argument, Romanyshyn made use of Merleau-Ponty's notion of flesh, described as "the *exemplar sensible . . . a general thing*, midway between the spatio-temporal individual and the idea, a sort of incarnate principle that brings a style of being wherever there is a fragment of being" (as cited by Romanyshyn, 2011, p. 46). Drawing from this concept, Romanyshyn argued that the primary door through which the characters of transference enter is the lived body of patient and therapist, and the particular style of being offered through flesh arrives through gesture. The gesture discloses a world, a clearing through which the individual expresses his or her history and fate, drawing in the other "flesh to flesh in a field of impregnation" (p. 50).

Romanyshyn (2011) has argued that the gestural body of the patient displays the leading edge of the transference. The character in the gesture of the symptomatic body asks, even demands, that the therapist respond to the patient's cast of psychological characters. The therapist is asked to give body to that which has been lost and unsuccessfully mourned. To effectively work through the transference, the therapist must "help the patient create a new body of understanding by creating with the patient an-other gestural field" (p. 52).

A significant portion of therapeutic process centers on creating a language to contain and make meaning of psychic experience. Psychotherapists generally neglect the fact that meaning is always already a body, a certain shape, movement, tone, color, and tension of flesh, and whereas words are bound to lead astray, flesh is always true to the psychic figures for whom the individual has sought treatment. Attending to the flesh in gesture allows the therapist and patient to mutually monitor the subtle shifts made by the otherwise invisible figures in the room. The compromise expressed through the symptomatic body is allowed a more direct expression and thus a possible resolution. The figures that carry the symptom are differentiated and mourned, no longer plaguing the lived body of the patient, a move from gross to subtle. The symptomatic image in the flesh is heavy, dense, and unrefined. When met with a mimetic expression through word and movement, the flesh can be crafted into a more subtle and livable embodiment.

## Guiding myths or mythic guides

As a psychology of pluralism, archetypal therapy attends to the multiple styles that can shape the transference dynamic. Lopez-Pedraza (1977) noted: "For our study of archetypal psychology we have to bear in mind that all the different Gods, within their different archetypal psychologies, each have his or her own way of transference" (p. 22). Because transference is always mythologically situated, arising out of the particular style of one god or another, the archetypal therapist must be familiar with mythological motif as it relates to human experience. In the remainder of this chapter I will review particular elements of classical mythology as it has been understood through the lens of archetypal psychology, ending with a case example that is aimed at exemplifying an archetypal understanding of psychodynamics.

## *Psychopathology and mythology*

As noted in the introduction to this study, inherent to every god is a particular style of healing and infirmity. Archetypal psychology has taken up the project of re-visioning pathology by seeing through the various maladies that fill the consulting room and psychiatric hospitals. Jung's (1939/1954) affirmations that "every psychic process is an image and an 'imagining' " (p. 544), and every image is shaped by an archetypally constituted complex (Jung, 1934/1960), has led archetypal theorists to conclude that every pathological expression has at its core a mythic figure.

This conclusion, and the archetypal re-visioning of myth and psychopathology that has proceeded from it, is not an attempt to create a new nosology, as if we could replace the Diagnostic and Statistic Manual with classic mythology. Rather, the move toward differentiating the mythic dimension of pathology has been conducted with the aim of exciting the imagination by bringing the fantasy of diagnostics back into contact with its primary source, "for how else can psychology as it is now conceived awaken to itself" (Hillman, 2007, p. 158). From an archetypal perspective, a mythic approach to diagnosis and formulation could never become a static nosology because "myths do not ground, they open" (Hillman, 2004, p. 20).

Archetypal psychology has taken seriously Jung's (1929/1968) argument that image is psyche. As such, psychopathology, the sufferings of psyche, are conceived to be illnesses of the image, or perhaps more accurately a sickness of the relationship between ego and image. Specifically, when a narrative ossifies into a rigid account of how things are, the individual forgoes receptivity to the multitude of imaginal possibilities, which from a mythic perspective means failure to propitiate the many gods in favor of the one with whom the individual has identified. Just as Orpheus was violently torn to pieces by maenads for his sole worship of Apollo, the psychically sick individual has built up a chronically narrow perspective and has become torn apart by those perspectival possibilities which have been hitherto precluded from life.

The archetypal therapist is a doctor of fantasy, making relative one fantasy by psychologizing or seeing through to its mythic root. As the god in the disease takes shape, the multitude of imaginal possibilities becomes more available, because, as Hillman (1975a) noted, "one instinct modifies another; one tale leads to another; one god implicates another" (p. 148). Differentiating the mythic figure prompts a process of crafting the diverse attributes of the symptom-image.

Archetypal psychology intervenes on the side of creative engagement with the archetypal determinants. The individual is responsible for refining the way in which these determinants presence themselves in his or her life. This refinement takes place in and through imagination, one essential aspect being how the therapist formulates the patient's material. In pursuit of archetypally informed formulations, archetypal psychologists have turned to the classical mythology of Greece to further illumine the way in which these stories shape life vis-à-vis the psychodynamics of the individual. Archetypal psychologists have explored the psychological implications of many myths and many gods. A complete review of this body of work is beyond the scope of this study. In the following section, I will explore aspects of the myths and mythic figures that I have found to have the most relevance for psychotherapeutic process.

## *Archetypal case formulation*

Christine Downing (2006) argued that depth psychology began with Freud's waking realization, "I am Oedipus." In reflecting on a series of dreams he had one year after his father died, Freud saw through to the underlying mythos that was shaping his psychological experience. He realized that what felt most private, dangerous, and taboo was at the same time a universal drama within which each human being must find his or her way. This monumental realization had profound effect on psychotherapeutic method, expanding the breadth of case formulation from a personalistic view of diagnosis and prognosis to a mythic understanding of the individual. By finding the Oedipus in his patient, Freud located himself in a place with significant therapeutic traction where the otherwise enigmatic idiosyncrasies of the patient fall into place as part of an Oedipal constellation.

Jealousies, rivalries, ambivalent feelings towards one's parents, regressive sexuality—these phenomena were all given place as quintessential features of the Oedipal situation.

Freud's move from observing psychic phenomena, such as dreams, symptoms, and behaviors, to locating these phenomena in a particular myth is what drew Jung's attention to Freud and became the seed from which Jung built his formulation of an archetypal unconscious. Jung (1912/1967) wrote:

> By penetrating into the blocked subterranean passages of our own psyches we grasp the living meaning of classical civilization, and at the same time we establish a firm foothold outside our own culture from which alone it is possible to gain an objective understanding of its foundations.
>
> (pp. 4–5)

The foundation of the psyche is most clearly represented in history, and more precisely in mythology—the imaginal history of humanity. Jung's method of amplification was built on this premise, as is one of the central therapeutic methods of archetypal psychotherapy: reversion. Exemplifying this point, Hillman (2005) wrote:

> Our lives follow mythical figures: we act, think, feel, only as permitted by primary patterns established in the imaginal world. Our psychological lives are mimetic to myths.. .. The task of archetypal psychology, and its therapy, is to discover the archetypal pattern for forms of behavior.
>
> (pp. 179–180)

As noted elsewhere in this study, locating the personal within the archetypal facilitates the profoundly therapeutic move towards valuing one's experience, including one's pathology. The recognition of the god in the disease shifts the fantasy from one of hero/victim battling with or helplessly suffering through life to a fantasy of living one's fate and crafting one's character in mimetic relation to the archetypal figures of imagination. Without reversion, psychopathology remains personalistic, forcing the person to carry the weight that rightfully belongs to a god. In an unpublished document, Hillman (1975c) noted: "Not only is the idea or text or image freed from its personal and historical associations, its knownness, but the soul by freeing becomes freed and returns to its source." The liberatory quality inherent to reverting the personal to the archetypal is mythically depicted in the metamorphosis of Narcissus from narcissistic inflation to the flowering of the imaginal.

## *Narcissus*

Narcissistic disorders have received explicit attention in psychoanalytic literature since Havelock Ellis (1897/2007) used the term as a synonym for auto-eroticism; however, as Hillman (1979) has noted, Narcissus himself has been largely precluded from the study of narcissism. Removed from his imaginal context and made into an "ism" of psychodiagnostics, Narcissus has been limited to a singular implication, severed from the myriad insights available in Ovid's tale, including the prospective, or final cause of this mythologem, which Hillman (1979) has considered nothing less than the formation of love for soul.

As an archetypal pattern, refining one's relation to the Narcissus motif is not a task limited to those who suffer from a narcissistic character disorder. The story of Narcissus presents the universally experienced negotiation between love of self and love of an-other. Ovid's tale offers mythic insight into the vicissitudes inherent to the movement from a primitive instinctual love of self to the development of a psychological relationship to others, the world, and to soul.

Nathan Schwartz-Salant (1986) has noted that the dynamics of narcissus are one aspect of the puer-senex constellation. Hillman's (2005) work on the puer has also noted this parallel. He described the puer as "narcissistic, inspired, effeminate, phallic, inquisitive, inventive, pensive, passive, fiery, and capricious" (p. 50). As noted above (Chapter 1), the puer has an affinity with the high-flying spirit, reluctant to come down from the flight of abstract intellect and spiritual pursuit to relate to psyche and world. According to Schwartz-Salant (1986), in treatment puer dynamics take "the inverse of the classical view of individuation: It goes from the top down, so to speak, from being concerned first with spirit and then with instinctual and shadow issues" (p. 21).

Ovid's Narcissus offers important insight into the way in which the puer may find the metaphorical ground he needs to establish himself as a robust psychic figure. As Hillman (2005) noted: "The collapse and fall into the world of soul-making as well as the wounds that attend upon puer perfection and high-flying ambition are structurally embedded in myths" (pp. 163–164). Narcissus demonstrates the puer's propensity toward a self-induced undoing from which grows a more precise sense of where to direct his thirst.

After chasing deer into his nets all day, Narcissus was drawn to a reflective pool, described by Ovid as:

> Limpid and silvery,
> Whither no shepherd came nor any herd,
> Nor mountain goat; and never bird nor beast
> Nor falling branch disturbed its shining peace;
> Grass grew around it, by the water fed,
> And trees to shield it from the warming sun.
>
> (Ovid, trans. 1986, pp. 391–429)

Narcissus was drawn by his consonance with this body of water, so similar to his own virginal body, echoing back to him an image of untouched purity that he both cherished and clutched. He was charmed by the quiet pool—pulled by his thirst to enter this *temenos*, a reflective space where puer and psyche meet in what Hillman (2005) described as the puer-psyche marriage. Hillman noted:

> The puer-psyche marriage results first of all in increased interiority. It constructs a walled space, the *thalamus* or bridal chamber, neither peak nor vale, but rather a place where both can be looked at through glass windows or be closed off with doors.
>
> (p. 88)

Sealed off from the chase/flee pattern so familiar to Narcissus, his thirst falls into the hands of *Pothos*, brother of Eros, who reflects back to Narcissus a "longing for that which cannot be obtained" (Hillman, 2005, p. 182). Pothos is a central player in the puer's movement from the lofty heights of self-involvement into relatedness. Stimulating a relentless cascade of fantasy, the *prima materia* of psychic reality, Pothos pulls spirit into psychological engagement and provides the necessary energy "so that we may go on loving" (p. 184).

As Narcissus gazed into the pool, he lamented the unquenchable nature of his desire. Longing and wounding became self-same, disclosing the inseparable nature of pothos and pathos. "In his grief he tore his robe and beat his pale cold fists upon his naked breast" (Ovid, trans. 1986, pp. 464–500). Like the fall of Icarus, the wounding of the puer carries forward his initiation into psychological life.

The psyche takes on a necessary split between pursuer and pursued, and as Hillman (2005) noted "*awareness of this doubleness of individuality is precisely the initiation*" (p. 189). He added:

> This initiation does not make us whole; rather it makes us aware of always being in a syzygy with another figure, always in a dance, always a reflection of an invisible other. Whether the other be senex to puer, female to male, mother to child, death to life in whatever form the other is constellated from moment to moment—*it is beyond reach*. . . . The other is an *unattainable image,* referring not to *himeros* [physical desire] and *anteros* [answering love], but to *pothos*. Or rather, the other is an image that is attainable only through imagination.
>
> (p. 190)

Narcissus offers a quintessential reflection of the doubled nature of puer consciousness. His longing pulls him out of himself and into the other. He breaks the virginal surface of the reflective pool, dipping his arms into the water where they find the moisture of relationship.

Moore (1994) described water as Narcissus' birthright and his special essence. In the act of deeply seeing water, Narcissus was looking into his familial lineage—his mother, a water lily, and his father a river god whom he likely never knew. His encasement in an impenetrable fixity (neurosis) was transmuted by seeing through his history and heritage, catching sight of the wavering translucent image that was his own otherness—the mercurial accompaniment of the double.

At the beginning of the tale, the mother of Narcissus asks Tiresias, the blind seer, if her son will have a long life, to which he replies "if he shall himself not know" (Ovid, trans. 1986, pp. 326–356). This prophetic foreshadowing essentially links self-knowledge and death. Importantly, Tiresias was one of the few allowed to retain his blood soul in Hades' underworld. Tiresias held death in life and found life in death. He knew that self-knowledge was in fact knowledge of the soul, and as Jung (1956/1970) noted, this kind of knowledge is always a death for the ego (p. 546). The self-enclosed impenetrability that would indeed grant Narcissus protection from the many deaths inherent to relatedness was ruptured through the tremendous pain associated with love. This love requires a two-ness; Narcissus had to differentiate out of primitive wholeness, Freud's (1914/1957) primary narcissism, and face the tremendous desire for the reflection of the other, without which he was left to feel utterly empty and worthless.

### *Kuhut's Narcissus: The deficient child*

Kohut has presented a compelling and clinically useful depiction of the phenomenology of a narcissistic disorder, particularly the emptiness or deficit that characterizes particular forms of narcissism. However, as I have noted, his observations have only a marginal relationship to the Narcissus myth. Kohut's emphasis on the deficiencies from early development, which continue to plague the adult, indicates that his reading of narcissism is not through Narcissus but rather through the archetype of the child; the deficiency at the center of Kohut's psychology is the tragedy of the abandoned child (Hillman, 1975b).

From an archetypal perspective Kohut has conflated the actual child with the mythical child. Jung (1950/1969) noted: "In psychological reality . . . the empirical idea 'child' is only the means . . . by which to express a psychic fact that cannot be formulated more exactly" (p. 161). The failure to differentiate the actual from the archetypal has led to an inflated view of childhood—"the cult of the child" (Hillman, 1975b, p. 18). The memory of childhood has been conflated with the reminiscences of the imaginal. As such, the imagination of psychology remains locked in fantasies of the child, tracking origins, evoking regression in service of the ego, and theorizing linear paths of development.

Kohut's psychology, rooted in fantasies of the tragic childhood, loses therapeutic efficacy by straying from the tragic genre to which it lays claim. The Kohutian approach imagines that with enough reparation made through transmuting internalizations and empathic reflection, the deficit with which one lives can be filled. Tragedy becomes comedy, tension relieved. Ironically, this effort to fill in the deficit, to change the child, is an effort to be rid of it once and for all (Hillman, 1975b). Hillman has argued that the cry of the child is an archetypal necessity and the tragedy of the *memoria* of childhood is an archetypal determinant: it must remain true to form as tragic: "We might imagine the child's abandonment and need for rescue as a continuous state, a static necessity that does not evolve towards independence, does not evolve at all, but remains as a requirement of the fulfilled and matured person" (p. 31). From an archetypal perspective the child must be lived in the present, by offering psychic space for its dependency, sensitivity, need for help, infantile wishes, omnipotent fantasies, and longings for merger.

### Demeter and Persephone

As Downing (2006) has noted, there are many essential links between the tale of Narcissus and the story of Demeter and Persephone. Downing has observed the way in which both stories take up the problem of enclosure from the world, when the protection which once served one well becomes a wall that must be, often violently, torn down, ushering in an initiation into relation with soul and world. Whereas Narcissus was bound up in a self-enclosed state, Persephone was enclosed in her mother's arms, bound by a bond that was broken by Hades, indicating once more the relationship between self-knowledge and death. To know herself as Queen of the underworld, Persephone had to die to her mother and lose the world she knew.

The *Homeric Hymn to Demeter* has brought image and narrative to the universal dynamics that unfold between a mother and a daughter, offering a wealth of meaning for the psyche of women. However the relevance of this myth is not confined to one gender. Karl Kerényi has considered the Demeter–Persephone motif to be one of the most significant myths for all of humanity (Downing, 1998). In *Eleusis: Archetypal Image of Mother and Daughter*, Kerényi (1967) has argued that the depiction of loss between Demeter and Persephone is characteristic of the loss each individual comes to experience as he or she is pulled out of the original fusion with the mother, a dependence of such intensity it led Donald Winnicott (1940/1992) to argue "There is no such thing as a baby; there is a baby and a mother" (p. 82).

Downing (1981) has supported Kerényi's argument by citing the "cult of the two goddesses" (p. 37), the Eleusinian mysteries of ancient Greece, where men and woman alike came to find initiation into the knowledge of these two distinct powers: Mother and Maiden. She noted that for the duration of the ritual, men took on names with a feminine ending, suggesting that the initiation involved an intensification of the feminine aspect of the human psyche.

As depth psychology has come to fill the significant emptiness left by the initiatory traditions, psychotherapists have been inducted into the role of transmitting the many mysteries of the soul. The analyst conducts analysis, a word that is cognate with the word loosening, implying that analytic work aims to loosen the rigid places of the psyche, allowing the soul to find its way through the initiatory process more directly. Often this loosening involves pulling what was one into two through the third. Differentiation, severing the lesser *coniunctio*, interpreting dependency and enmeshment, the optimal frustration of the analytic situation, metabolizing projective identifications, these are all acts in which loosening, separation, and thus loss occur. The *Homeric Hymn to Demeter* depicts the most profound of these necessary separations and opens several modes of imagining the loss.

As Downing (1981) has noted, in Homer's *Hymn to Demeter*, we meet Persephone through the perspective of Demeter. It is her loss, pain, and anger that the reader encounters most directly. Demeter provides an essential image of depression, essential because, as archetype, she carries both pathology and cure. As Berry (1994) has noted:

> "like cures like" . . . once we recognize an archetypal pattern, we know a great deal about curing it. That is, we treat it with itself—by deepening it, expanding it (so that it is no longer so narrowly fixated), and by giving it substance, body (so that it can now begin to carry what it is trying to express).
>
> (p. 197)

Berry goes on to note that the symptom expresses its final cause (Jung), but does so through a compromise (Freud) in a way that attempts to prevent the goal from ever being reached (Adler).

Homer has clearly depicted the mythic expression of grief: the scorched earth bereft of life by Demeter's curse, the desperate appeals she made to the Gods for their assistance, her attempts to annul her loss with another child, her isolation, loss of appetite, and refusal to be consoled. The loss of an-other is, as Freud (1914/1957) argued, experienced as a loss to the self. Demeter's attempts to cover over the full implications of her loss is perhaps most evident in her commitment to nurse Demophoön whom she "anointed with ambrosia like one born from a god and breathed sweetly on him" (Homer, trans. 2001, p. 240). Demeter was crafting a fantasy child. Her attempts to make him immortal reflect the melancholic's adhesion to an eternally abiding internal object. She was attempting to bring back that part of herself that was lost when Hades took her daughter. Nursing Demophoön was a compromise between her profound desire to regain what she had lost, a wish fulfillment, and the full realization of the implications of her loss, a nearly intolerable thought.

Following the telos of the myth, one finds that a Demetrian depression is connected, through her daughter in the depths, to the underworld of Hades. Demeter, Goddess of life, harvest, and grain met her winter through her daughter's rape, and thus the giver of seasons learned intimately of the loss that is connected with life. In response to this feature, Berry (1994) extrapolated the following implications:

> When in tune with Demeter and receiving her gifts, I must also expect some of the accompanying difficulties and unconscious tendencies of that archetype. Then, too, my need will be always to deepen teleologically in the direction of Hades, my daughter's realm. Thus I suffer, and yet thus I also resist—for that too is part of my mythic pattern. There is no way *out* of a myth—only a way more deeply into it.
>
> (p. 199)

One finds in Demeter a sense of familiarity, her expression of loss so close to what we all know from experience. Demeter, Goddess of harvest, earth, and grain, is one face of our clinging to life and our hatred for all things underworld, especially death. Demetrian depression draws her thick cloak tight and blocks out the underworld perspective, obscuring the psychological significance of loss. Demeter's loss is only literal, and her rage at Hades for taking her daughter obfuscates the riches that he always brings, prevents her from turning her gifts of growth and vegetation into psychic growth and vegetation (Berry, 1982). Loss has no redemption.

Demeter's period of depressive isolation began to shift as she found herself relating to a group of caring women. The pinnacle moment in this transition came through the penetrating force of humor. Old Baubo staged a dance for Demeter, in which she lifts her skirt and comically displays her vulva. This unexpected move cracks through Demeter's rigid adherence to self-destruction, bringing her back into relation with the world around her. As Downing (1994) noted, Baubo "is often represented seated on a pig, legs outspread, holding a ladder upright in her hand" (p. 240). She offers a way out through the upward movement of laughter. Just as a laugh begins deep in the belly and cascades itself upward through the body, entering into the world in a melodious song, Baubo reaches down into the depths of the depression, lifting the skirts of secrecy and rumination, and finds a way to make us laugh at the foolishness of it all.

## *Psychic rape*

Homer's *Hymn to Demeter* begins with a seemingly mundane moment—a young woman picking flowers in a field with her mother standing at a distance. After the rape, however, reflection shows a scene of such perfection, one's heart aches to be back in that place. Homer's depiction sets the scene in a field abundant with life—the flowers and the maidens together, a perfect image of the virginal psyche filled with a quality of "in-one-selfness" (Downing, 1981, p. 38), a quality one only experiences through the backward glance of imaginal reminiscence. The rupture has always already occurred. The untouched perfection, the maiden-with-flowers-and-field quality, often as it may appear in fantasy, is only a preliminary to the inevitable loss. All parts of the myth are necessary, and one is never without the other—perfection and loss inextricably bound.

Homer's depiction of this necessity comes through an unusual, that is, important, collusion between Zeus and Earth. Gaia, a mother in her own right, "grew as a snare for the flower-faced maiden in order to gratify by Zeus's design the Host-to-Many" (Homer, trans. 2001, p. 10). Gaia knows the necessity of rape (Berry, 1982).

The self-same flower that forms the penultimate image of the Narcissus myth as well as his namesake is used to lure her in. The rape of Persephone is constellated as she gripped the narcissus, or one might say, by the grip of her narcissism (Berry, 1982). The Persephone of the field, virgin maiden, suffered from her lack of suffering, protected by the all-giving hand of her mother. Without the rupture of Hades, Persephone was fixed in an enclosed fusion, devoid of three dimensionality.

Berry (1982) addressed the therapeutic treatment of Demeter-Persephone motifs. She noted the negative implications of interpreting the rape as " 'a destructive animus' or 'negative shadow' " (p. 27). To do so would miss the necessity of the rupture and loss of innocent virginity. Hades, loss, and death are essential psychological experiences, particularly when the individual has been limited by a fused relationship with the mother. "The 'rapist' may be constellated in response to the dreamer's too narrow virginity, and his purpose may be to escort her physically into that deeper body, which lies beneath all surfaces, the psychic realm" (p. 27).

Demeter defenses can easily dominate a therapeutic treatment as well. One might imagine a successful psychotherapeutic treatment as the appropriate combination of binding and unbinding, life and death (Levin, 2002). Demeter resists the necessary death of meaning, the states of unknowing, the loss of the familiar. When attention is focused primarily on gathering, culmination, harvest, Hades is forced to work from the underground, devising ways to pull the earth out from underneath the treatment.

### *Oedipus*

Psychological reflections on the parallels between Narcissus and Persephone show the way in which these stories form a mythos of initiation into love through death, the move from enclosure to the formation of identity through relationship. Similarly, we might consider the tragedy of Oedipus as reflecting a different aspect of this same problem, as if the three myths were different facets of the same gem. Freud (1914/1957) described narcissistic love as an intermediary stage between complete self-enclosure, where the other does not yet exist, and the stage in which the individual has accomplished love of the object. Downing (2006) described this state of primary narcissism as representative of "the fantasy that separation is not the ultimate truth, that to begin with we were whole in ourselves and at one with the world" (p. 312). There can be no loss because there is no emotional investment outside oneself. Narcissistic love is a love of self as object. Embedded in the Narcissus motif are the challenges one has to meet in order to achieve that love of self that arrives through love of soul in Hillman's (1975a) sense of the notion.

Alternatively, Freud (1910/1960) argued, the way in which we live out the Oedipus myth shapes our capacity to love an-other. The point of contact, where the two facets meet, is the depiction of the profound loss inherent to the separation between oneself and the object of one's love whether it is a love for self, that is, the fantasy of primary narcissism, or the love for mother, that is, the incest fantasy. As Downing (2006) has noted, our turn to the other in the Oedipal dynamic is in response to the loss of primary narcissism. She wrote, "Our initial turn to an other expresses our impossible longing for this other to give us back this lost wholeness. It is really an expression of fusion longing, expresses a desire to *be*, not to *have*" (p. 312). She added,

> Only, we might say, when we acknowledge the existence of a rival, admit that the mother does not exist only in relation to us, only as we enter the Oedipal world, does the possibility of real loving, of Eros, emerge.
>
> (p. 312)

The story of Oedipus, like Narcissus, illuminates the tragic nature of longing, that what we long for is a fantasy, out of reach and prohibited in the deepest sense. For Freud, the Oedipal world was marked by mourning and ambivalence: "We are passionately attached to those on whom we are dependent *and* passionately resentful of that dependence" (Downing, 2006, p. 288).

Jung, in his move away from what he considered Freud's literalistic reading of Oedipus and his overemphasis on sexuality, reinterpreted the incest motif in terms of the pull one feels to cultivate a dynamic relationship with the deep unconscious. Jung (1912/1967) wrote "in actual psychic experience the mother corresponds to the collective unconscious, and the son to consciousness, which fancies itself free but must ever again succumb to the power of sleep and deadening unconsciousness" (p. 259). Jung argued that the "son of the mother" (p. 259) will always die young, but the hero can overcome the negative mother-imago, slaying the dragon, freeing himself from a merged relationship with the unconscious.

He considered the appearance of the incest motif to be an indication that the individual had been initiated into a movement towards individuation. Jung (1946/1966) argued: "Whenever this drive for wholeness appears, it begins by disguising itself under the symbolism of incest, for, unless he seeks it in himself, a man's nearest feminine counterpart is to be found in his mother, sister, or daughter" (p. 263). For Jung, incest was an early manifestation of what would become, with the development of the capacity for symbolic thinking, a vital relationship to the mythic unconscious.

Hillman (2007) argued that Freud's adherence to a mythological formulation of human behavior, his insistence that we are Oedipus, has brought about a culture-wide initiation into the Oedipus tragedy, inextricably shaping the way in which we see our history. He noted: "Early years and repressed memories are so fateful, in our culture, because psychoanalysis dominates our cult of souls and Oedipus is the dominant myth practiced in the cult" (p. 161). Freud's development of a psychoanalysis based on his insight into this myth positioned Oedipus as the ruling figure, the archetypal dominant of psychoanalytic practice. Incest, parricide, and the tireless pursuit of truth through reductive reasoning are the bedrock for much of psychoanalysis. Although these features may help organize and clarify the patient's experience, Hillman argued that there are other features of this myth that have found their way into analytic practice, features which, when unrecognized, may prove destructive to therapeutic treatment.

Hillman (2007) has interpreted the central problem in the Oedipus myth not as incest and parricide but literalism. He argued that both Laius and Oedipus fail to see the second meaning in the oracles. They took them as literal and so fell under their sway. This negation of metaphor, Hillman suggested, is represented in the myth by the motif of infanticide. Laius, emblematic of the rigid king defending his claim, was threatened by the possibilities presented by a new child—the archetypal personification of imaginative possibility. His response was to bind the child's feet and leave him to die on Mt. Cithaeron. If Hillman is correct in placing Oedipus as the primary archetypal dominant of analysis then both patient and therapist will always be, in one form or another, in relation to this infanticidal motif, killing off the second sense by clinging to a singular myth and systematic interpretations.

## Case example

### *Preamble*

The following summary of the patient's history and treatment is, like all clinical vignettes, a fantasy. I have collected the patient's biographical nodal points and particular therapeutic insights and authored them into a narrative. The result is a literary product that helps me, as clinician, to imagine the patient's psychological dynamics and to learn from my experience in the treatment. But, it also has the potential to blind me to alternative formulations—different ways of imagining. Despite the inherent limitations that come with case history, formulation, and treatment summaries, reflections such as these are an essential aspect of psychotherapy. One distinguishing feature that sets archetypal case formulation apart from those typically encountered in the field of psychology is the move towards relativizing the case history as a fictional account—an attempt to write a healing fiction (Hillman, 1983).

### *Case history and formulation*

Mr. C was a 33-year-old, European-American male, an only child raised by a single mother. His father left home before he was born, and Mr. C has never met him. From an early age Mr. C had a strong passion for playing drums. He received his first drum set when he was seven years old and started taking lessons at 10. In his teens he practiced four to six hours a day. He often reminisced about his pattern of regularly skipping out on class so that he could stay home and practice music. When his mother found out, she responded by getting him enrolled in an independent home-based program so he could both pursue his passion for drumming and finish high school.

Mr. C spent 10 years in the military serving as a combat medic, beginning at age 18. Twice in his service he was deployed to serve in war. At the time of our initial meeting Mr. C was a college student working on a degree in biology. He had completed three full-time college years and was looking to do an internship during the upcoming summer.

Mr. C relied heavily on a hyper-masculine style of consciousness, marked by emotional insensitivity and excessive rationality. His emotional life and connection to his imagination suffered under his profound rigidity. The assuredness and intellectual prowess Mr. C displayed to the world covered over a wealth of anxiety and doubt. When discussing his depression, he noted that one of the things he was disturbed by was his lack of trust. He added, "I feel like I don't know people well enough to share thought cycles and emotions that are illogical or bizarre." His psyche was rich with fantasy, yet, bound by the fear of rejection, he kept his images sealed within his very private and compartmentalized psyche.

Mr. C presented as a hard working individual with intense self-expectations. For example, he noted that one of the things he struggles with the most is "staying competitive." Statements such as these stimulated my own questions about the missing father—imagining his fascination with competition as a puer-driven push to win the father's pride and attention. Schenk (2001a), following Hillman, noted "[The puer] is representative of a search for spirit in the form of the sky father and a yearning to redeem the father by surpassing him" (p. 79).

When Mr. C experienced failure, he was overtaken by senex-like self-criticism, guilt, and self-punishment. This in turn aggravated his anxiety, which arrived as physical tension, trouble sleeping, and upset stomach. When his level of depression was high, Mr. C described a tendency to be retiring, shy, aloof, timid, and inhibited, but also irritable, high-strung, and impatient. Throughout our time together, Mr. C described a pervasive fear of rejection, hunger for an understanding other, and deeply seated anger stemming from the psychological isolation in which he was living.

His relationship with his mother was thoroughly colored with shades of the hero/son–great mother motif. The enmeshment he described was a prominent theme throughout his life. He often fought against the merger by attempting to "slay the dragon"[1] through his anger, overt rejection of his mother, and a misogynistic attitude towards women. In addition, the war he waged against his father fed his punitive and distrusting attitude. Like King Laius, father of Oedipus Rex, Mr. C was terrified of losing his kingdom to the new child, so he made regular practice of killing off potential space with his extreme criticism and skeptical style of consciousness.

### *Reflections on therapeutic approach*

Mr. C came to therapy to work on his depression and his inability to trust. In our initial session, he described his depressive symptoms, pronouncing each word as if it were made of lead. His heavy description collected on the floor of the consulting room, gradually forming a dense wall between he and I. Corroborating this vivid image of separation, Mr. C began describing his long-standing sense of isolation and a pattern of paranoid retreat into solipsistic fantasy. The wall of words kept him trapped in his own bizarre world where his vulnerability and emotionality was protected/imprisoned by a leaden shield.

In imagining his personality from a diagnostic perspective, he clearly fit the criteria for a schizoid personality disorder. Psychoanalytic practitioners would likely take up the developmental origins of his character and manifestations of his pathology in the transference. Laplanche's (1997) theory of seduction would suggest that the emotions and fantasies that haunt his mind are remnants of a primal seduction, which as an infant, Mr. C was unable to translate, or signify. Early in his development, these remnants ossified into an internalized object, an enigmatic signifier, which stimulates "a permanent excitation of the infant's instinctual semiotic functioning" (Levin, 2002, p. 138). The barrage of fantasy and "bizarre" emotions were an attempt to "translate the untranslatable fragment" (p. 138).

From this Laplanchian perspective, the treatment would aim at binding "images and symbols in meaningful, stable structures" (p. 142) and unbinding the crystalized narratives that have become pathogenic. Laplanche has argued that some of these fragments remain untranslatable, continually exciting fantasy "like an indigestible piece of metal lodged in the stomach" (Levin, 2002, p. 138).

In his formulation of the seduction theory noted above, Laplanche (1999) took a strong stance against structuralist theories, arguing that the fantasies of the individual are utterly idiosyncratic; there is no "need to refer to the archetypal and the unconscious of the species" (p. 156). Whereas a Laplanchian approach would likely foster significant therapeutic traction, an archetypal approach conjoins the differentiation and analysis of the idiosyncratic fantasies and symptoms with a process of seeing through the personal pathology to the mythic backdrop, thus placing personal development within a significantly broader context rich with imaginative possibility. Rather than focusing primarily on tracking Mr. C's fantasies back to developmental roots and interpreting the way in which his paranoid isolation comes up in the transference, archetypal psychotherapy would attend to vivifying the imagination of the wound. What characters are at play here; how are they at work in the room; and how is he resisting their influence?

An archetypal perspective contends that the images that populate the psyche do indeed have an integral relationship to our bodily experience with others in the world, but they are also archetypal in nature. The style in which they cluster together is mythopoetic. As such they can be brought into symbolization through an epistrophe, a reversion, not necessarily to the early life of the individual, but to the early life of humanity—those timeless stories that we have told for the very purpose of crafting meaning, giving language to that which is otherwise untranslatable. The therapeutic effect of such a move is one of value. What seems utterly personal is in fact transpersonal and has been happening since time immemorial.

As noted above, Levin (2002) likened the untranslatable fragments to bits of metal lodged in the digestive system, resisting the psyche's tireless attempts to break it down. One might argue, however, that the image he used to qualify this experience carries with it significant "need to refer to the archetypal" (Laplanche, 1999, p. 156). In broadening the context of investigation, we find that the untranslatable fragment is an age old, i.e. archetypal problem—what alchemy has referred to as the stubborn poison, "the old remainder, the lead, the raven, the black sludge left over" (Hillman, 2005, p. 274). Hillman noted "the most recalcitrant encrustations of the complex, its oldest habits . . . are neither childhood remnants nor parental introjections but senex phenomena, that is, *the structure and principles by which the complex endures*" (p. 274). For an alchemical psychology, the indigestible metal is "the focus to which its operation returns again and again . . . the senex component of the complex" (p. 274).

Alchemy offers much in terms of insight regarding the transmutation of metal. For alchemy the digestive metaphor would only be one operation among many. The metal of alchemy required not just solution in acid but a multitude of different activities, including grinding, rotting, heating, cooling, drying, moistening, and combining with other substances, each move stemming from careful attention to the dynamics of the material. The operations outlined by the alchemists add significant complexity to the digestive metaphor used often in psychoanalytic theory. Without recourse to the archetypal nature of the psyche, the insight of alchemy and other such mythopoetic traditions remains largely dormant, only to be rediscovered piecemeal through the analyst's intuitive moves.

### Treatment

Early in the treatment, Mr. C shared a fantasy of a King on a throne lamenting the scorched earth that had become his kingdom. He remained in this image for several sessions, touching on the various ways his psychic situation lacked fertility. He described the way his depressive thoughts dominate his mental space, precluding any new growth, the way his relationships all felt cold and sterile, lacking the sparks of inspiration that could be built up into a flame of Eros. Together, we investigated the way in which both he and I had felt this infertility in the treatment. As he found language to name "the unthought known" (Bollas, 1989), the lamenting King began loosening his grip, and Mr. C slowly developed the ability to see the image as a distinct phenomenon, separate from, but related to, himself.

His attention then shifted to focus on his "absurd emotional thoughts" and "absurd insecurities." He noted his extreme sensitivity to criticism, and his frequent attempts to avoid confrontation. He told many stories in which he compulsively distanced himself from relationships. When he did find closeness with someone, the intimacy they shared was limited by his defensiveness and difficulty being vulnerable.

Halfway through the treatment he had a fantasy of a little kid on a playground surrounded by a group of bullies. They were hitting him and taunting him for being different. I noted that this fantasy was essentially the other side of his lamenting King. The fertile spark of the puer was trapped in a circle of bullies, encased in the shame these figures had beat into the little boy. Mr. C's chronic distrust of others, his supposition that the care he feels from others is inauthentic, was stemming from his anticipation that there is a group of bullies in every person waiting for him to become vulnerable so they can attack his weakness.

Despite movement in some areas, Mr. C continued to believe he was, as he often noted, "seeing the world objectively." He had an arsenal of examples he would use to defend his perspective, to "exteriorize issues away from the psyche" (Hillman, 2005, p. 276). The senex quality in Mr. C's psychology was intent on locating the problem outside of himself. His paranoia, although tyrannical and destructive, gave him a sense of order from which he could make sense of the world. If he were to allow room for the perspective of the puer, this order would be disrupted, and he would have to encounter the turmoil of psychic ambivalence and conflict.

The domination of the senex was preventing the life-giving link between eros and psyche (Hillman, 2005, p. 277). When a puer spark managed to penetrate through the thick crust of senex consciousness, it was quickly extinguished, preventing any opportunity for the generativity that arrives with psychological reflection on puer inspirations. Rather than fostering the erotic process of meaning making, these inspirations were a source of tremendous anxiety. Through the dark lens of the negative senex, his feelings and fantasies, rich with meaning and psychic creativity, were perverted into "absurd emotional thoughts" and "absurd insecurities."

Without psychological reflection, his anxiety had no other mode of expression but somatic symptoms: physical tension, nervousness, trouble sleeping, and upset stomach. Commenting on the psyche-soma relationship, Jung (1935/1976) wrote the following:

> The psychic fact and the physiological fact come together in a peculiar way. They happen together and are, so I assume, simply two different aspects to our mind, but not in reality. We see them as two on account of the utter incapacity of our mind to think of them together.
>
> (p. 65)

His defensive expression of psyche as physical symptom was an effort to maintain the split to which Jung referred. However, like all neurotic symptoms, his physical symptoms were both defensive and expressive. His bodily complaints were an expression of the "depth in the surface" (Schenk, 2001b, p. 20), conveying psychological meaning through aesthetic presentation.

With consistent attention to the dynamics of his physical symptoms, we were able to reestablish ourselves in a more direct relationship with his psyche through image. The upset stomach was imagined as a boiling cauldron of anger. The tension he felt in his body was like sheets of desert rock, his nervousness like a frayed electrical wire. These images emerged through a simple process of sticking with the symptom and following its analogical richness through associations. The symptoms were windows looking out into Mr. C's psychological cosmos, his imaginal *polis*—the figures that had been there all along shaping his thoughts, feelings, behaviors, and dreams.

Several months into the treatment, Mr. C presented the following dream:

> *A man with a big machete is chasing me through an open field. He wants to cut off my arms. I am terrified, so I keep running as fast as I can. No matter how fast I run, he remains right behind me.*
>
> (Client's dream, July 8, 2009)

The link between running and being chased gave rise to a close look at the way his running necessitates a chase, the way he distances so others with pursue. I pointed out the play between the words chased and chaste. This opened a discussion of the connection between his desire for perfection and the lack of fertility he feels in relationships.

This discussion allowed us to ease into what I thought to be the most important aspect of the dream—the Dionysian dismemberment. As Downing (1993) has noted, Dionysus dissolves boundaries, and his appearance "is always experienced as threatening, as overpowering, as *epidemia*" (p. 69). The dream ego, terrified and running, is representative of a typical response to the Dionysian influence. However, in order to understand what this image was offering, we had to relativize the terrified-I of the dream, treating it as an image distinct from Mr. C's waking consciousness.

We had already qualified this "I" as chased and chaste, running for perfection, terrified of losing his arms. Playing with the pun, he likened the image of losing his arms to dropping his primary weapons, his self-critical attitude and his paranoid fear that others will exploit his vulnerability. He began to acknowledge the value of this Dionysian figure and the importance of being dismembered. More broadly, he had an experience in which his perspective shifted from "the psyche, like the rest of the world, is out to get me" to the recognition that this figure that invoked such terror, both in the dream and upon waking, was actually arriving with a certain fateful necessity, inflicting death so that life could continue.

This experience was central in building his psychological faith, which, as Hillman (1975a) noted,

> begins in the love of images, and it flows mainly though the shapes of persons in reveries, fantasies, reflections, and imaginations. Their increasing vivification gives one an increasing conviction of having, and then of being, an interior reality of deep significance transcending one's personal life.
>
> (p. 50)

Several months after he had the dream, Mr. C had a fantasy in which he was running through the open field of his dream. Suddenly he came to a stop, turned toward the man with the machete, and watched pensively as this man cut through his arms. He described looking down at his flesh laying in the field and reflected on how his arms, that which he used to arm himself, would decay and decompose, becoming life-giving fertilizer for this open field. He likened this image of fertility to the opening of psychological possibilities. The field became a field of imagination from which a multitude of potentials could emerge. Mr. C lived with this dismembering quality in a variety of ways, the most prominent of which was his growing ability to pull apart his senex paranoias and self-attacking fantasies.

## Notes

1 Jung (1912/1967) and Erich Neumann (1954/1995) described the needed separation from the personal and archetypal mother as the heroic task of slaying the dragon.

## References

Berry, P. (1982). *Echo's subtle body: Contributions to an archetypal psychology.* Putnam, CT: Spring.

Berry, P. (1994). The rape of Demeter/Persephone and neurosis. In C. Downing (Ed.), *The long journey home: Re-visioning the myth of Demeter and Persephone for our time* (pp. 197–205). Boston, MA: Shambhala.

Bion, W. R. (1962). The psycho-analytic study of thinking. *International Journal of Psycho-Analysis*, *43*, 306–310. Retrieved from http://search.ebscohost.com/login.aspx?direct=true&db=pph&AN=IJP.043.0306A&site=ehost-live

Bollas, C. (1989). *The shadow of the object: Psychoanalysis of the unthought known*. New York, NY: Columbia University Press.

Corbin, H. (1997). *Alone with the alone: Creative imagination in the Sūfism of Ibn Árabī* (R. Manheim, Trans.). Princeton, NJ: Princeton University Press.

Davidson, D. (1966). Transference as a form of active imagination. *Journal of Analytical Psychology*, *11*, 135–147.

Denis, P. (2005). Transference. In A. D. Mijolla (Ed.), *International Dictionary of Psychoanalysis* (pp. 1776–1778). New York, NY: Macmillan Reference USA.

Downing, C. (1981). *The goddess: mythological images of the feminine*. New York, NY: Crossroad.

Downing, C. (1993). *Gods in our midst: Mythological images of the masculine—A woman's view*. Putnam, CT: Spring.

Downing, C. (1994). Hekate, Rhea, and Baubo: Perspectives on menopause. In C. Downing (Ed.), *The long journey home: Re-visioning the myth of Demeter and Persephone for our time* (pp. 197–205). Boston, MA: Shambhala.

Downing, C. (Speaker). (1998). *Creative Mythology*. [Cassette Recording, No. 1–5]. Santa Barbara, CA: Pacifica Graduate Institute.

Downing, C. (2006). *Gleanings: Essays 1982–2006*. Lincoln, NE: iUniverse.

Ellis, H. (2007). *Sexual inversion: A critical edition*. New York, NY: Palgrave Macmillan. (Original work published 1897)

Freud, S. (1957). On narcissism: An introduction. In J. Strachey (Ed.), *The standard edition of the complete psychological works of Sigmund Freud* (Vol. 14, pp. 73–102). London: Hogarth Press. (Original work published 1914)

Freud, S. (1960). A special type of choice of object made by men. In J. Strachey (Ed.), *The standard edition of the complete psychological works of Sigmund Freud* (Vol. 6, pp. 163–176). London: Hogarth Press. (Original work published 1910)

Freud, S. (1977). *Introductory lectures on psychoanalysis*. (J. Strachey & G. Zilboorg, Trans.). New York, NY: W. W. Norton. (Original work published 1916)

Freud, S. (1981). The dynamics of transference. In R. Langs (Ed.) *Classics of psychoanalytic technique* (pp. 3–8). New York/London: Jason Aronson. (Reprinted from *The standard edition of the complete psychological works of Sigmund Freud*, *12*, pp. 97–108, by J. Strachey, Ed., Trans., 1953–1974, London: The Hogarth Press and the Institute of Psycho-analysis) (Original work published 1912)

Freud, S. (2004). *Studies in hysteria*. (J. Strachey & G. Zilboorg, Trans.). New York, NY: Penguin. (Original work published 1895)

Hillman, J. (1972). *The myth of analysis*. Evanston: Northwestern University Press.

Hillman, J. (1975a). *Re-visioning psychology*. New York, NY: Harper and Row.

Hillman, J. (1975b). *Loose ends: Primary papers in archetypal psychology*. Putnam, CT: Spring.

Hillman, J. (1975c). Modes of thought. [Unpublished notes]. The James Hillman Collection (A75b, 108). OPUS Archives and Research Center, Carpinteria, CA.

Hillman, J. (1979). *Dream and underworld*. New York, NY: Harper and Row.
Hillman, J. (1983). *Healing fiction*. Berrytown, New York: Station Hill Press.
Hillman, J. (1989). From mirror to window: Curing psychoanalysis of its narcissism. *Spring*, *49*, 62–75.
Hillman, J. (2004). *Archetypal psychology*. Putnam, CT: Spring.
Hillman, J. (2005). *Senex and puer*. Putnam, CT: Spring.
Hillman, J. (2007). *Mythic figures*. Putnam, CT: Spring.
Homer. (2001). *The Homeric hymn to Demeter*. (S. L. Harris, Trans.). Mountain View, CA: Mayfield Publishing.
Jung, C. G. (1954). Foreword to Suzuki's introduction to Zen Buddhism. In H. Read, M. Fordham, G. Adler, & W. McGuire (Eds.), *The collected works of C. G. Jung* (R. F. C. Hull, Trans.) (Vol. 11, pp. 538–557). Princeton, NJ: Princeton University Press. (Original work published 1939)
Jung, C. G. (1960). The real and the surreal. In H. Read, M. Fordham, G. Adler, & W. McGuire (Eds.), *The collected works of C. G. Jung* (R. F. C. Hull, Trans.) (Vol. 8, pp. 382–384). Princeton, NJ: Princeton University Press. (Original work published 1933)
Jung, C. G. (1960). A review of the complex theory. In H. Read, M. Fordham, G. Adler, & W. McGuire (Eds.), *The collected works of C. G. Jung* (R. F. C. Hull, Trans.) (Vol. 8, pp. 319–337). Princeton, NJ: Princeton University Press. (Original work published 1934)
Jung, C. G. (1966). The practical use of dream analysis. In H. Read, M. Fordham, G. Adler, & W. McGuire (Eds.), *The collected works of C. G. Jung* (R. F. C. Hull, Trans.) (Vol. 16, pp. 139–161). Princeton, NJ: Princeton University Press. (Original work published 1934)
Jung, C. G. (1966). The psychology of the transference. In H. Read, M. Fordham, G. Adler, & W. McGuire (Eds.), *The collected works of C. G. Jung* (R. F. C. Hull, Trans.) (2nd ed., Vol. 16, pp. 163–327). Princeton, NJ: Princeton University Press. (Original work published 1946)
Jung, C. G. (1967). Symbols of transformation. In H. Read, M. Fordham, G. Adler, & W. McGuire (Eds.), *The collected works of C. G. Jung* (R. F. C. Hull, Trans.) (2nd ed., Vol. 5). Princeton, NJ: Princeton University Press. (Original work published 1912)
Jung, C. G. (1968). Commentary on the secret of the golden flower. In H. Read, M. Fordham, G. Adler, & W. McGuire (Eds.), *The collected works of C. G. Jung* (R. F. C. Hull, Trans.) (Vol. 13, pp. 1–56). Princeton, NJ: Princeton University Press. (Original work published 1929)
Jung, C. G. (1969). Concerning rebirth. In H. Read, M. Fordham, G. Adler, & W. McGuire (Eds.), *The collected works of C. G. Jung* (R. F. C. Hull, Trans.) (Vol. 9i, pp. 113–150). Princeton, NJ: Princeton University Press. (Original work published 1950)
Jung, C. G. (1970). Mysterium coniunctionis: An inquiry into the separation and synthesis of psychic opposites in alchemy. In H. Read, M. Fordham, G. Adler, & W. McGuire (Eds.), *The collected works of C. G. Jung* (R. F. C. Hull, Trans.) (2nd ed., Vol. 14). Princeton, NJ: Princeton University Press. (Original work published 1956)
Jung, C. G. (1976). The Tavistock lectures. In H. Read, M. Fordham, G. Adler, & W. McGuire (Eds.), *The collected works of C. G. Jung* (R. F. C. Hull, Trans.)

(Vol. 18, pp. 5–167). Princeton, NJ: Princeton University Press. (Original work published 1935)

Kerényi, K. (1967). *Eleusis: archetypal image of mother and daughter*. New York, NY: Bollingen Foundation.

Klein, M. (1981). The origins of transference. In R. Langs (Ed.) *Classics of psychoanalytic technique* (pp. 9–15). New York/London: Jason Aronson. (Reprinted from *Envy and gratitude and other works* pp. 48–56, by M. Klein, 1975, New York: The Melanie Klein Trust) (Original work published 1952)

Kohut, H. (1971). *The analysis of the self: A systematic approach to the psychoanalytic treatment of narcissistic personality disorders*. Chicago: University Of Chicago Press.

Laplanche, J. (1997). The theory of seduction and the problem of the other. *International Journal of Psychoanalysis*, *78*, 653–667.

Laplanche, J. (1999). *Essays on otherness*. New York, NY: Routledge.

Levin, M. (2002). *The work of Jean Laplanche*. Retrieved from ProQuest Digital Dissertations. (AAT 3051891)

Lopez-Pedraza, R. (1977). *Hermes and his children*. Zurich, Switzerland: Spring.

Mitchell, S. A., & Black, M. J. (1995). *Freud and beyond*. New York, NY: Basic Books.

Mitrani, J. L. (1999). The case of 'The Flying Dutchman' and the search for a containing object. *International Journal of Psycho-Analysis*, *80*, 47–69.

Mitrani, J. L. (2001). 'Taking the transference:' Some technical implications in three papers by Bion. *International Journal of Psycho-Analysis*, *82*, 1085–1104.

Moore, T. (1994). *Care of the soul: A guide for cultivating depth and sacredness in everyday life*. New York, NY: Harper Perennial.

Neumann, E. (1995). *The origins and history of consciousness*. Princeton, NJ: Princeton University Press. (Original work published 1954)

Ogden, T. H. (1983). The concept of internal object relations. *International Journal of Psycho-Analysis*, *64*, 227–242.

Ovid. (1986). *Metamorphoses*. (A. D. Melville, Trans.). New York, NY: Oxford University Press.

Romanyshyn, R. (2011). The body in psychotherapy: Contributions of Merleau-Ponty. In R. A. Jones (Ed.). *Body, mind and healing after Jung: A space of questions*. New York, NY: Taylor & Francis.

Samuels, A. (1985). *Jung and the post-Jungians*. New York, NY: Routledge.

Schenk, R. (2001a). *The sunken quest, the wasted fisher, the pregnant fish: Postmodern reflections on depth psychology*. Wilmette, IL: Chiron.

Schenk, R. (2001b). *Dark light: The appearance of death in everyday life*. New York, NY: State University of New York Press.

Schwartz-Salant, N. (1986). *Narcissism and character transformation: The psychology of narcissistic character disorders*. New York, NY: Inner City Books.

Segal, H. (1964). *Introduction to the work of Melanie Klein*. New York, NY: Basic Books.

Segal, H. (1983). Some clinical implications of Melanie Klein's work—Emergence from narcissism. *International Journal of Psycho-Analysis*, *64*, 269–276. Retrieved from http://search.ebscohost.com/login.aspx?direct=true&db=pph&AN=IJP.064.0269A&site=ehost-live

Singer, E. (1970). *Key concepts in psychotherapy* (2nd ed.). New York, NY: Basic Books.

Van den Berg, J. H. (1961). *The changing nature of man*. (H. F. Croes, Trans.). New York, NY: Dell.

Van den Berg, J. H. (1972). *A different existence: Principles of phenomenological psychopathology*. Pittsburgh, PA: Duquesne University Press.

Wiener, J. (2010). Working in and with transference. In M. Stein (Ed.), *Jungian psychoanalysis: Working in the spirit of C.G. Jung* (pp. 78–90). Chicago, IL: Open Court.

Winnicott, D. W. (1992). *The child, the family, and the outside world*. New York, NY: Da Capo Press. (Original work published 1940)

Wolstein, B. (1954). *Transference: Its meaning and function in psychoanalytic therapy*. New York, NY: Grune & Stratton.

Chapter 4

# Word and image

Hillman (1975) has argued that words are the carriers of soul, insisting: "They are personal presences which have whole mythologies: genders, genealogies (etymologies concerning origins and creations), histories, and vogues; and their own guarding, blaspheming, creating, and annihilating effects" (p. 9). In a powerful rejection of the nominalism common to modern philosophy of the West, Hillman has made language psychological by affirming "words are persons" (p. 9), and their presence strongly influences the nature of psyche. This position brings a necessary renewal to the notion of a talking cure, encouraging the clinician to carefully attend to the words used in session—vivifying the image present in the word.

In his efforts to further explicate an archetypal perspective on language, Coppin (1996) undertook an important investigation of the discrepancy between a depth psychological theory that argues for the inherent multiplicity of the psyche while continuing to use a style of language that connotes monolithic singularity and reification. In an effort to depict a style of language that better reflects the polycentric nature of the psyche, Coppin argued for the following: "Language," he wrote, "can best be seen as a living autonomous figure of psyche" (p. 82); however, psychotherapy suffers from a pattern of using language to reduce, objectify, and tame the images of psyche. A more psyche-centered approach involves using language to express the concrete qualities of the images. The images presented by the patient provide the primary material for the therapeutic encounter, and the psychotherapist can help evoke images by positioning him or herself in an imaginal or waking dream state, speaking to the patient with a sense of play. For example, sound associations, neologism, and repetition often help highlight the imaginal, that is, the metaphorical and multifarious nature of language (p. 84).

## Language of the particular

As I have noted throughout this text, one of the primary aims of an archetypal psychotherapy is the careful differentiation of the psyche in its multitude of expressions. Significant importance is given to the assumption that the psyche's most fundamental expression is image. As such the words used in therapy are intended to bring these images forward. Language is used to clarify the particular qualities of the presenting image. This move requires the participants to first bracket their habitual subjectivity and allow the image to speak its qualities. Lockhart noted "one of the ego's subtle influences is to generalize what it sees in the *other*" (as cited in Coppin, p. 91). This tendency to generalize can quickly pervert an entirely new expression of the psyche into something that is already known by the patient, therapist, or both. The ego responds with anxiety in the face of the unfamiliar, not trusting the significant therapeutic import of that which is unknown.

An archetypal approach works to counter this tendency by giving value to the peculiar and subtle detail of the image. Lockhart argued,

> one's exact fate and individuality are tied to those details . . . the unknown and unrecognized details that are not readily comprehended or understood must not be forgotten. What is more to the point is to be silent in the face of them and let *them* speak.
>
> (as cited in Coppin, 1996, pp. 91–92)

The patient and therapist slowly elucidate a depiction of the details of the image, allowing, when appropriate, for gaps in the verbal content so that both individuals have the time and privacy for reverie, resting in the cloud of unknowing.

Postmodern philosophers, most notably Jacques Derrida (1974) and Ludwig Wittgenstein (1953), have argued that language will always force experience into an already known referential reality, or as Derrida (1974) noted, "there is nothing outside of the text" (p. 155). Each word uttered only carries meaning in relation to and in contrast with other words. The postmodern view of language has significant implications for psychotherapy, where language is arguably the most central component. The linguistic prison described by postmodern philosophers induces a pessimistic view regarding the possibility of surprise that arrives as conceptual systems and conventional discourse are momentarily shattered. In summarizing

Wittgenstein's view, Sanford Drob (2008) wrote: "any gesture toward a transcendental signified is, like a move in the game of chess, only comprehensible as such within a context, a form-of-life/language game that provides it with sense" (p. 157).

In the same essay, Drob (2008) has argued that archetypal psychology has crafted an argument that shows more optimism in relation to the problem of language. He wrote:

> By relentlessly writing outside the ruling discourse, by imploring us to stick with our uninterpreted experience and images, and by creating new metaphors that deconstruct and expand our conception of the psyche, Hillman has battled against the view that "truth" or "reality" is defined simply by how these terms function in our conventions and prevailing theories.
>
> (p. 160)

Hillman (1975) has posed the argument that words are not, necessarily, policemen on the prowl but can actually be used in a way that breaks through pre-established systems of meaning, like using a thorn to remove a thorn. He argued "the true iconoclast is the image itself which explodes its allegorical meanings, releasing startling new insights" (p. 8).

To "reach beyond a linguistic prison of our own creation" (Drob, 2008, p. 165) requires a shift in awareness from one's typical subjectivity to the things themselves. Hillman has described this way of attending as *notitia*: "that capacity to form true notions of things from attentive noticing" (as cited in Coppin, 1996, p. 114). This is a move away from collapsing experience into a narrative of the "I." Instead, the therapist and patient move into the world of things and their respective qualities. Hillman has referred to this as an "adjectival revolution"—"a return of the secondary qualities to things—colors, textures, tastes" (p. 114).

The practice of notitia is reflected most directly in the archetypal style of dream work. The moves made with the dream are primarily centered on elucidating the qualities and states of the various images as independent entities unto themselves. The work of interpretation may ultimately relate back to the dream ego and the waking ego, but prior to doing so, the dream is afforded the time and space necessary to understand the images in their own right. This involves stepping into the variety of perspectives presented by the images: not as representations of the multiple sides of the waking ego, but as autonomous entities distinct from the dominant style of consciousness. This same move is extended out to the therapeutic encounter in its entirety, where the images of the dayworld are also approached through the paradigm of dream with the affordance of autonomy and metaphorical significance.

A patient noted that throughout his week he felt as if he had just dropped a handful of bb bullets. They had spilled out wildly on the ground, and he was frantically attempting to pick them all up. As he said this, his speech was pressured and rapid. He quickly moved onto another association. As he paused, I brought his attention back to the image. Although "the I" was a primary feature in this image, I tried not to assume that he and I knew this figure or that it was the same "I" that was currently sitting across from me. I directed his attention to the image by asking him what this "I," this dropping bb bullets figure, looked like. My reference to "the figure" and "this I" is a simple but essential move in structuring a dialogue that reflects the plurality of the psyche. He quickly replied "he looks like me," evidencing the ego's desire to stay with what is known. I asked him to go to the image of the "I" and describe him as if he were talking with a blind person. His speech, breathing, and gestures slowed as he vocalized the details of the image. The figure began to grow in complexity, wild hair, large rapidly moving eyes, sweaty forehead, flailing arms. As he picked up one bb, several more fell from his hand, as if the bbs were resisting his efforts to gather them. With the emergence of these details, he was able to differentiate this figure from the observing "I" with which he was currently identified. *Dropping the bbs* and *the frantic "I"* became important images for his treatment. Through taking time to notice and differentiate the image, we developed a shared language for a complex that had brought him tremendous difficulty throughout his life.

The image this patient presented was immediately accessible to an imaginal approach largely because he had already personified his experience. Such experiences are not infrequent in psychotherapy; however, the therapist can enhance this primary mode of image-making by modeling a style of language that aims at personifying. Coppin (1996) has clearly described the intent of personifying language.

> In summary we can say that personifying means giving subjectivity to things through speech. For example, we might change

> the phrase, "I really have the blues," into "The Blues sure do have me." In this sentence the Blues are subjective. . . . Hillman suggests this as a linguistic move that relativizes the ego and animates the psychological world.
>
> (p. 115)

The therapist vivifies the personified image in the sentence by reversing the subject and object. This is particularly important with feelings. In highlighting the personified presence of the feeling, the therapist and patient animate the feeling, placing the patient "in a more receptive and fluid position relative to experience" (p. 116).

Hillman (1975) has described the therapeutic traction one gains through the use of personifying language. He noted,

> what was once an affect, a symptom, an obsession, is now a figure with whom I can talk. In Jung's sense we are reversing history in our souls, for by personifying I restore to the disease its God and give the God its due.
>
> (p. 34)

Here Hillman has pointed to the notion that the symptom seeks fulfillment. It requires some kind of expression and action. In mythological terms, the Gods have been offended and reparation is required through an embodied deepening of the particular style one has disavowed.

## Entering the dialogue

In the course of a session patients often shift into a different style of dialogue, evoking in the therapist a palpable feeling that a different character has entered the room. Perhaps it is the tone, the ideological position, the pace, gesture, or any of the other ancillary features of communication. The therapist attends to these shifts and draws attention to them. With attention and care, these subtle shifts can develop into highly differentiated characters, accentuating the diversity of the patient's psyche.

Coppin (1996) has highlighted the way both Watkins and Hillman follow the language of the patient and listen for the images already embedded in his or her speech. For Watkins, these images become the guiding metaphors for the treatment. She described her approach as an attempt to "hold the images from their dreams and their active imagination so that when we're talking about different things that are coming up in their life it is those images that we can see the events through" (Coppin, 1996, p. 125).

Hillman described the way in which he listens to the speech of the patient and reflects back to him or her what has been said while giving the phrase "a *fresh twist*, in which the therapist gives images back to the patient with a slight, but noticeable shift" (Coppin, 1996, p. 117). Following Berry (1982) one might imagine this move as mimetic to the style taken up by Echo. In her anger, Hera cursed her speech: "When speaking ends, all she can do is double each last word, and echo back again the voice she's heard" (Ovid, trans. 1986, pp. 357–390). Echo's brilliance is in the way she takes what has been said and finds the play in words, so that she can express her desire. She is limited in speech, but this limit gives her vocalizations tremendous impact. "It chanced Narcissus, searching for his friends, called 'Anyone here?' and Echo answered 'Here!' Amazed he looked all round and, raising his voice, called 'Come this way!' and Echo called 'This way!'" (pp. 357–390).

The generative quality to Echo's speech reverberates throughout the story. Berry (1982) has noted that Echo's dialogue with Hera was concealing the erotic encounter between Zeus and the nymphs. Her words "make possible . . . a certain covert fertility" (p. 116). The therapist offering a fresh twist to the words of the patient makes accessible the procreative power in the word, the metaphors which are always already embedded in language because all language originates out of the poetic basis of mind.

## Archetypal linguistics

Kugler's (1982) study entitled *The Alchemy of Discourse* has been instrumental in further elucidating the mytho-poetic foundation from which language is formed. His exposition began by placing Jung at the forefront of the discovery of the unconscious dimension that is embedded in language. Jung's early experiments with word association led him to conclude that as an individual's attention decreases, that is, as he or she becomes more unconscious, associations become increasingly based on phonetic structure as opposed to syntactic structure. In addition, phonetic associations, which are based on sound, cluster together forming a meaningful complex, a sound-image, reflecting a layer of the psyche where logos and image are innately connected. Kugler used the example of the "flower complex," which consists of the words *fl*ower, de*fl*ower, and de*fl*oration; *car*nation, *car*nal, and *car*nage; *vio*let, *vio*late, and *vio*lent. Whereas these words do not carry a meaningful syntactic or etymological relationship, "the pure relations between the sounds" (p. 52) do in fact carry an archetypal image-meaning.

The flower complex described above is depicted quite clearly in Homer's *Hymn to Demeter*. As was described earlier (Chapter 3), Persephone, virgin maiden, was gathering flowers in the field. Just as her hand grasps the most beautiful of the flowers, the earth violently opens, and Hades takes the captured Persephone back to his underworld realm to complete his act of violation. This motif shows a gathering of the phonetically related words, brought into a meaningful relationship through an archetypal fantasy (Kugler, 1982).

Jung's research, which corroborates statements made by Freud (1900/1953), Jacques Lacan (1953/1981), Ferdinand de Saussure (1916/2011), Claude Lévi-Strauss (1958/1983), and Theodore Thass-Thienemann (1973), has documented the two levels of language operating synchronously. Kugler (1982) has described the utility of the manifest level in the following statement: "The metonymic functions by concatenating words into linear chains according to the laws of grammar and syntax" (p. 109). This is the language of the ego, where meanings are constricted to singular form. While the ego shapes reality into a singular fantasy, there is another process operating, in which events are experienced as polysemous. Kugler described this as "the metaphoric operation in language" which "associates words according to some degree of phonetic and or semantic (identity or analogy) parity, not syntactically" (p. 109). This level of experience has been referred to variously as primary process (Freud, 1900/1953), fantasy thinking (Jung, 1912/1967), the symbolic order (Lacan, 1953/1981), and poetic basis of mind (Hillman, 1975). It is the linguistic structure of what depth psychology has called the unconscious, an "interior archetypal thesaurus, a psychic dictionary which imaginally binds together archetypally related meanings through a parity of phonetic values" (Kugler, 1982, p. 103).

As the ego fixates on one meaning, the ulterior meanings are relegated to expressions outside one's field of awareness, represented most directly as the persons of our dreams. Neurosis, according to Jung (1950/1969), is one-sidedness, the ego's overly fixated condition, cut off from the vitalizing effect of "our imaginal otherness" (Kugler, 1982, p. 100).

As I have noted throughout this study, a primary aim in archetypal psychotherapy is the reconstitution of one's relationship to the imaginal, the relativization of the ego and its linguistic style, by seeing through and hearing through the ego's presentation to the underlying "multiplicity of meanings within the physiognomy of [his or her] own soul-image (imagination)" (Kugler, 1982, p. 93). The unconscious meaning, however, does not arrive through the therapist's translation from metaphoric to metonymic meaning, such is the work of ego psychologies. As Berry (1982) has demonstrated, interpretations that translate the image are always going to be relative to the particular perspective with which the therapist has identified. Archetypal psychology has advocated an approach to the image that favors multiplicity of meaning over any single truth. The move could be described as a shift from strengthening the ego through fostering a cohesive narrative to strengthening the poetic basis of mind through initiation into the many narratives of the archetypal psyche. Kugler (1982) has noted the way in which the archetypal psychotherapist works to keep the meaning in the image, retaining its poetic fecundity, by allowing the dreamer's words "to speak for themselves through their inherent polysemy" (p. 93). This approach was reviewed in detail in Chapter 2.

Kugler (1982) summarized his study in the following statement:

> A lowering of consciousness shifts the linguistic mode of association from a consideration of the meaning-concepts associated with the objects of reference to a consideration of the meaning-concepts connected through phonetic parity to the object's signifier—its phonetic pattern. *This process involves freeing the soul (the meaning concept) from its imprisonment in matter (the literal object of reference).*
>
> (p. 117)

Kugler's assertion has significant implications for the way in which a therapist attends to the patient in psychotherapy. If attention is focused, concentration high, then the therapist's own internal associations will be largely syntactic, singular, and ego-based. Conversely, if the therapist allows his or her attention to soften, associations will be comprised of a blend of both syntactic and phonetic, egoistic and imaginal.

In the privacy of his or her own mind, the therapist is encouraged to make space to play with the linguistic image offered by the patient, space for reverie where subjective and objective meanings blend, and words can fill out into their imaginal form. From this place of evenly-suspended attention (Freud, 1900/1953), or reverie (Romanyshyn, 2002), the therapist has opportunity to hear the stale language of pathology and offer back to the patient a "fresh twist" (Coppin, 1996, p. 117) to what has been said.

Kugler's (1982) study on the archetypal basis of language culminates in an exposition on the alchemy of discourse. He noted the way in which the alchemists understood how words connect through sound and highlighted their reliance on the play between the subjective and objective meaning of the word. For example, Kugler noted the double meaning of the word solution: an answer to a problem and a liquid substance. Here we have two completely different objective referents, related only through phonetic relationship. However, the alchemists found value in the link, working through their subjective problems as they worked through various transformations of a liquid substance. Kugler noted "*the acoustic image is the crucial intersection between the external and internal, between the literal and metaphoric*" (p. 113).

The archetypal psychotherapist works to see through the ego's literalistic style of language to the archetypal image embedded in the phonetic elements of the words used. Each word carries with it associational links to other words, not only through meaning but also through sound. Every word arrives already in a myth, an archetypal image that transcends the idiosyncrasies of the individual and the individual's particular language. By learning to recognize and relate to the archetypal syntax of imagination the patient is given an opportunity to experience his or her fundamental immersion in language, that through words we find ourselves always already in a sea of patterns and meaning, that each utterance is archetypally constituted, that beneath the singularity of egoistic speech is an "inherence of the angel in the word" (Hillman, 1975, p. 9), and from such experiences one comes to develop a profound respect for the depth, mystery, complexity, and richness of the psyche.

## The language of metaphor

Archetypal psychology has made significant use of language borrowed from particular disciplines that have specialized in concrete qualitative differentiation, such as the art of memory, mythology, and alchemy (Hillman, 1975). In a brief essay transcribed from a lecture in Zurich, Hillman (1980b) has described alchemical language itself as a mode of therapy. Hillman begins this exposition with a discussion of the connection between language and neurosis, stating "the one-sidedness which characterizes all neurosis in general is also to be found specifically as a one-sidedness in language" (p. 119). By implication, this means that the phenomenology of the neurosis is to be found in "the style of speech in which the neurosis is couched" (p. 119). Therapy of psyche becomes therapy of words; the archetypal therapist directs the treatment towards rectifying the loss of the metaphorical sensibility in relation to language—a reconnection between words and their imaginal root.

Hillman (1975, 1980b) has argued that an alchemical psychology keeps the metaphorical sensibility alive by using image-words like salt, sulphur, and mercury—poetic descriptions of personality. Image-words bring a constellation of qualities and context. Alchemical language, Hillman (1980b) asserted, provides an alternative to the dry abstractions of psychological textbooks. The use of terms like ego, unconscious, and transference abstract from the lived experience of the psyche and sacrifice therapeutic precision. Hillman has called for a rectification of psychotherapy through the therapeutic use of alchemy's concrete metaphors and qualitatively differentiated language.

## Toward an alchemical psychotherapy

The following section provides a descriptive review of Hillman's work on alchemy. The principle aim of this review is to gather together the most clinically useful aspects of Hillman's alchemical psychology and to continue his overarching effort to highlight the way in which the metaphors embedded in alchemical language constitute a lexicon more psychological than conceptual language. As Hillman (1980a) noted, "The poetic basis of mind implies that the psychology of mind will have to find its way into poetic speech" (p. 46).

Arguably, Hillman's most clinically relevant contribution to poetic speech is found in his work with alchemical color symbolism, which has drawn attention to the way in which the dynamics of the psyche and their vicissitudes are reflected in the shades of the image. An alchemical psychotherapy invites careful attention to these shifts in shade, the transmutation of qualities, the flow of adjectives—a poetic re-visioning of psychodynamics.

### *Prima materia*

The first movement in the opus of alchemy or the work of psychotherapy is to locate the *prima materia*, a substance that is paradoxically hidden because it is everywhere, imagined as a variety of substances: virgin milk, mercury, dung, serpent, white smoke, death. More broadly, the prima materia is made up of that which spontaneously presents itself to imagination. Schenk (2006) drew analogies to the beginning moments of psychotherapy—"the encounter in the waiting room, the first look on the face, the initial words spoken. What is the face saying today? the body? the first words?" (p. 156).

The primary matter has also been described as a *massa confusa*, an undifferentiated mass, unconscious ambivalence, the moments in which one is moving in a multitude of directions at once, not sure where to turn, filled with doubt, desperation, and a sense of necessity. The anxiety of uncertainty inspires a desire to move towards coagulation, prematurely forcing this new experience into the pattern of something known and familiar.

Hillman (1980a) described the necessity of differentiating the whiteness of the beginning from the silvery whiteness of *albedo*. The virginal material is characterized by an "unworked innocence" (Hillman, 1980a, p. 24), the sinless, stainless, purity, which lacks the heat and flexibility that comes from working the material. The virgin white is pre-black, a state of unconsciousness, a participation mystique, going with the flow, the "no bad vibes" of California vernacular. This virginal white, like Persephone in the field of flowers, requires the death and putrification of nigredo, the pull of Hades into the soul's underworld.

To move the primary matter from its virginal state to the first stage of the opus, the nigredo, it is essential to reach further into the blackness that characterizes this stage of the work. The operations associated with nigredo, namely mortificatio and *putrefacatio* suggest the necessity of death. The raw material of the beginning has to die to its pre-reflective meaning then suffer a process akin to a slow grinding of substance with mortar and pestle, so that it may ferment and rot into a blackness that is blacker than black (Hillman, 1997). As Hillman noted "the nigredo is not the beginning, but an accomplished stage" (pp. 6–7).

## *Nigredo*

Although shadows are cast throughout the stages of the opus, as a general heuristic one might consider the most significant confrontation with the shadow as an essential feature of the nigredo. The symptoms of body, mood, and thought begin to speak, and their breath reeks of that which has been neglected and left to rot. The nigredo involves both a psychological digestion of the shadow as well as digestion by the shadow; that is, the psyche is infused with the logos of black. Black dissolves all other colors, and, as Hillman (1997) noted, "by absenting color, black prevents phenomena from presenting their virtues" (p. 8). The levity of spirit, the air of intellect, the lightness of laughter all become blackened, so spirit is deflated (the crash of Icarus), thought is fervently bleak, and the only laughter is that of bitter irony.

Hillman (1997) has described the deconstructive quality of the nigredo, taking what was fixed and dissolving its properties, making psychic space for a new paradigm. For space to emerge, one has to be able to see the experience of nigredo as an experience, not an identity. The alchemists imagined the essential move towards disidentification as a decapitation, which "allows the mind to recognize and thereby be freer from what the body feels" (Hillman, 1997, p. 11). This operation of *seperatio* creates a significant shift in the work, allowing psychic states to be related to as things-in-themselves, moving the opus along toward the silvery reflection of albedo.

## *Albedo*

In his two-part essay *Silver and the White Earth*, Hillman (1980a, 1981b) explicated an alchemy of the reflective function, referred to variously as the albedo, the silvering of the psyche, or anima consciousness. This is a mode in which "seeing, listening, attending all shift from the gross attachments of the nigredo," where matter and mental processes are split and material is dense and difficult, "to a new transparency and resonance. Things shine and speak. They are images, bodies of subtlety. They address the soul by showing forth their souls" (Hillman, 1981b, p. 25).

Hillman's (1980a) exposition of albedo describes with qualitative precision the psychic qualities of silver and its relation to imagination, pathology, and the other psycho-physical constituents of alchemy. Hillman has equated this middle stage between nigredo and *rubedo* with the in-betweenness of psychic reality. He also contrasted the painful stillness of nigredo, with the motion inherent to albedo. Whereas nigredo speaks of a past seemingly frozen and stuck, "albedo talk speaks rather of 'what's going on,' this move and that: how the psyche is moving and what moves the patient and the analyst make in response" (p. 33).

The movement from black to white may also become apparent in the moments when an individual's sense of inherent badness and inextricable guilt, "the bowels of *putrefactio*" (Hillman, 1981b, p. 33), dissolves into a state in which thinking can be generative. Memories are taken up with a sense of play. The fixity of nigredo ruminations give way to memory as image, that is, fluid, complex, and rich with a diversity of meaning.

Patients with severe early trauma may consistently reject the therapist's attempts at whitening their black memory. Having been severely affected by such experiences, they often need the memory to remain literal to justify their current psychological difficulties. To find play in the memory, the reflection of silver, would require the individual to begin to take responsibility for his or her psychical facts. In such situations, where the stuckness is nearly suffocating, Hillman (1981b) has offered the following suggestion:

> It seems that the best way to hold the blackest of the black—that irremediable and inert pathology—is again with silvered soul, that quality of understanding appropriate to the holiest of essences, that enlightened and compassionate mind which belongs to the white anima. Only she can distil from the utter blackness some trickle of possibility.
>
> (p. 29)

Bion labeled the raw sensory and proprioceptive data of the mind beta elements (β-elements). Because the severely traumatized patient alluded to above is incapable of digesting the intolerable image (Lopez-Pedraza, 1977) of psychic trauma, his or her mind is generally overwhelmed and requires a thinking, feeling therapist to digest the material. These β-elements are projected into the therapist who serves as the container for the undigested psychological material. Through a dream-like reverie the therapist takes in, processes, and empathically attunes to the material. Bion called this the alpha-function. This containment transmutes the material into an alpha element (α-elements)—a digestible experience that can be given back to the patient. The patient takes in the more tolerable α-element, which allows opportunity to think and feel the experience. Bion (1962) offers the following example:

> If the infant feels it is dying it can arouse fears that it is dying in the mother. A well-balanced mother can accept these and respond therapeutically: that is to say in a manner that makes the infant feel it is receiving its frightened personality back again, but in a form that it can tolerate—the fears are manageable by the infant personality.
>
> (p. 310)

Bion referred to this interchange as container/contained (♀ ♂). The container (♀) is essentially the object into which the β-element is projected, and the contained (♂) is the material that is projected out into the container (Bion, 1962).

The move from nigredo to albedo, or from β-element to α-element, should not be confused, however, with the absolving of psychic pain. Rather, the shift is from one kind of pain, a chaotic, rotting, infectious pain, to a pain of mourning. "Shadow . . . is not washed away and gone but is built into the psyche's body and becomes transparent enough for anyone to see" (Hillman, 1981a, p. 34). Such transitions arrive in gradations, passing, as Hillman (1981a) has noted, from the blacks to the blues, where one finds the poem in the pain, the quivering songs of the melancholic mood.

Hillman's (1981a, 2006) two essays on blue have aimed at differentiating this stage from the mortificatio period of the black. The nameless dread without space or time, the experience of soul death, shifts in blue to a depression with form and substance, lamentation and sorrow. From this perspective, depression is an indication of procession through the opus and a valuable experience unto itself. Hillman (1981a) has argued that blue "is the color of imagination *tout court*" (p. 39). He highlighted the following amplifications:

> the blue mood which sponsors reverie, the blue sky which calls the mythic imagination to its farthest reaches, the blue of Mary who is the Western epitome of anima and her instigation of image making, the blue rose of romance.
>
> (p. 39)

With the shift to blue, the psyche finds itself in the blues where reverie and imagination replace ego-fixation with a burgeoning sense of soul.

Importantly, the transition from black to blue to white does not adhere to a straight and steady path. The material can readily regress back to its blackened state, "the black crows creeping back down into the nest" (Hillman, 1981b, p. 21), or fall back into the powdery whiteness of denial, a move analogous to the alchemist throwing the material into the fire and closing the hatch. Hillman has advised clinicians to hold to prudent awareness when a whiteness appears, lest one mistake a flight into health for a true albedo. He suggested that one should bring body to the experience by sticking close to "those hidden forms within each of the manifest emotional changes that have led to the albedo" (p. 35). The images that present are the body of the albedo. They are the flesh of anima, the *axis mundi* of reflective consciousness, always indicating what is happening right now, thus providing a necessary relief from the seemingly endless iteration of past experience.

The respite of the albedo, however, can become a deterrent itself. Intensification of the fire of analysis is required in order to keep the engagement, a fermentation, which percolates the soul and brings a fresh wave of intensity. Without a proper heating of the material, vitrification may ensue. This has been described as a glassy impenetrability, where "insight coagulates into truth" (Hillman, 1981b, p. 40), and the material becomes sealed off from the multitude of perspectives present in the array of metals.

Vitrification is an experience of psychological density, where "a dog is a dog is a dog" (Winnicott, 1971, p. 33), psychic reality denied. Hillman (1981b) noted "nothing takes place until we can see through the fixed as fantasy and coagulate fantasy into forms and limits" (p. 40). A binary is set up between the literal-minded ego and the "problem" "out there" in "reality." Hillman quoted Mary the Jewess: "if the two do not become one, that is, if the volatile does not combine with the fixed, nothing will take place" (as cited in Hillman, 1981b, p. 40). The fixity of literalism has to combine with the volatility of psychic fantasy, allowing as Gaston Bachelard (1987) has noted in his description of the work of imagination, deformation, or contortion of sensate experience. When the imaginative work of deformation is kept separate from the material, the banal problems, the neurotic conditions, the relational impasses, it will remain fixed—"nothing will take place" (Hillman, 1981b, p. 40).

### *Silver*

Hillman (1980a) described silver as a metal of the moon, white or greyish in color and associated with the albedo stage of the alchemical process—"the lunification of the material" (p. 24), drying calcination, lustration, or coagulation. Reflective silver comes only after an extensive working of the material. It requires the heat of mental processes, turning intellect and sulphuric passion toward the psychic condition. When the reverse is true, when sulphur dominates silver, the reflective surface of the silver is blackened by the fervent sulphur, literalizing desires into burning action.

> Imagine this metal then as a nontangible whitened air, a silvering white body, ethereal like the orb of the full moon floating, suspended in dark azure receptivity, a hard, cool and bright mind at its full, whose effects are both nourishing as well as desiccating and astringent.
>
> (p. 24)

An astringent imagination cuts through the oily phlegmatic quality of an image, freeing its movement, releasing its pungency, producing a psychic experience that can be both sharply incisive and harshly biting or caustic.

The reflective whiteness of silver is the feminine counterpart to the active red or gold. The cool reflective properties of the moon compliment and contain the active principle of the alchemical gold. "It is the hard lunar mind, solid in the realization of its imaginative forms, which allows gold to be hammered into specific shape and take on definition" (Hillman, 1980a, p. 26). Without the qualities of silver, the gold that forms is a common gold, lacking the fineness of silver, the aesthetics of the insight, truth without beauty. Silver restrains the gold from the unbridled solar activity of the hero, "enabling the gold to recognize that it and all its power is held to the enactment of psychic images" (p. 30).

In his review of the relationship between silver and lead, Hillman (1980a) noted "a whiteness with the wings of a dove can emerge from a leaden state that seems completely to enclose it. The dull and heavy heart of lead conceals a dove of silver" (p. 33). Lead has its home in the heaviness of pathology, the sloth and torpor of depression, the unmovable dense facets of character. The silver that is concealed in the lead suggests that within an individual's most stubborn and fixed forms of suffering is a white dove, which, given the right provocation, will fly forth out of the leaden encasement, signaling a conciliatory peace and a reflective clarity between the pathologized leadenness and the struggling ego.

The stuckness of lead is where the silver is mined. The silver contained within the lead implies that the reflective insight and the depression are intrinsic to each other. Pockets of soul are located by finding areas where lead has stopped the forward movement—the hang-ups, hesitancies, fixations, and melancholic moments of daily living.

The necessary polishing of the silver comes through the *iteratio*, the repetition of the content within the rudiment of the treatment. The covering over of one's reflective capacity, through shame, literalism, denial, projection, is clarified through interpretation, empathic reflection arising from the silver of the therapists mind, and the slow differentiation of the psychic condition. However, the tarnished silver of cloudy reflection may serve an important purpose, allowing "the right embodiment which cannot occur until the soul succumbs fully to Luna" (Hillman, 1980a, p. 40). Deepening into the particular kind of lunacy that has gripped the individual allows the psyche time to bathe in its own reflection, from which it can return to earth with a sense of the realness and reliability of the image.

Streams of silver may also be mined through the fleeting images of fantasy. Here we see the relationship between mercury and silver. The quicksilver in the silver makes these moments pass by without pause or reflection, masking the pithy poetics of reverie and daydream. Mercury quickens the silver, mercurializing its reflection, connecting the mining of silver to both rapid and unpredictable change as well as thievery. Reflective moments must be stolen out of the quick moving flow of image, the participation mystique of the virginal psyche. Conversely, Benedictus Figulus, a sixteenth-century alchemist, noted "Mercury can be animated only by the white ferment of silver" (as cited by Hillman, 1980a, p. 27). "The God and guide of the whole opus" (p. 27) becomes animated, that is alive, only through "mental ferment, the animation of thought and reflection, the active intervention of imagination" (p. 27).

Silver is the alchemical material by which one may experience the resonance and re-sounding of a patient's material, like the fresh twist and word play described above. Hillman (1980a) described the silvered ear as "the art of hearing musically, letting the word resound, as the Second Musician plays upon the First Musician's silver sound of music, doubling the meaning, catching an additional inflection from the words" (p. 43). The second sounding implied in the re-sounding is the underworld of the word. Just as the ancient Greeks imagined that death incited a separation of the psyche from the body, the second sound of silver marks the liberation of the image from the material referent to which the word was bound. "This ear hears for rhetoric, for rhythm, sound, breath, and silence; for evocation of psychical essences . . . so that everything said or read matters to the soul because it bears psychic matter" (p. 44).

### *From white to yellow*

The transition from white to yellow happens by means of sulphur. Sulphur's adhesive substance brings the mind out of the resonate reflections of silver and into relation with the desired object (Hillman, 1991), a process analogous to Freud's (1933/1964) notion of cathexis. It binds the mind to an object through emotion, and its fire is akin to the sticky passions of libidinal energy. Sulphur has a second side. In *Mysterium Coniunctionis*, Jung (1956/1970) described sulphur as related to both conscious will and unconscious compulsion. In either form, it brings the individual out into the world, into action.

This intermediary between white and red, the yellowing or *citrinitas*, is an action that has been subject to the many deaths and fermentations of nigredo and the imaginal insights of albedo, producing an ever increasing heat felt in the return of emotionality, the dawn just before the sunrise of rubedo. Whereas the stirrings of passionate action during the nigredo or albedo may reflect a defensive posturing against the pain of black or the chilly coolness of silver, the yellowing of the work marks a needed shift from the *unio mentalis*, the union of soul and spirit, toward a meeting of soul in body and world. Jung noted the redemptive quality of rubedo initiated by the *citrinitas*: "in this state of 'whiteness' one does not *live*. . . . In order to . . . come alive it must have 'blood' . . . the rubedo, the 'redness' of life. . . . then the opus magnum is finished" (as cited by Hillman, 1991, p. 91).

Hillman (1991) has used his exposition of the *citrinitas* to criticize psychoanalytic theorists and practitioners for their fixation on the psychological reflection of albedo, noting that as long as one remains in this stage of the work, the problems of the world will be reduced, through interpretive measures, to the projections of the patient. In turn, he noted, "we believe magically that self-transformation trickles down (multiplies and projects) into the world" (p. 93).

Although his essay on the yellowing of the work marked Hillman's formal announcement of his move away from private practice psychotherapy and thus serves, in some regard, as a supporting argument for this significant transition, his admonishment against the unequivocal subjectivizing of every anxiety, particularly the patient's stated concerns over the incessant destruction of the world, is a profoundly important critique of psychotherapeutic practice. Further attention will be given to Hillman's turn to the world in the following chapter.

### *Rubedo* or the goal of the work

Hillman's (1993) essay on the final stage of the alchemical opus, the rubedo or philosopher's stone, characteristically aims to deliteralize the notion of goal as a linear development from one place to another. Rather, Hillman argued, each alchemical operation, each image, is itself a goal, complete in its own right. For example, the telos of the seemingly endless ruminations of the nigredo, the scouring over of one's early life, the search for cause and condition, is ultimately the recognition of the hand fate has played. The goal is right there in the bare facts of one's life, requiring not a change in substance but a change of mind.

The goal is both ever present and always allusive. The essential feature of the alchemical goal is not its attainment, but the idea. Jung made this clear: "the goal is important only as an idea; the essential thing is the opus which leads to the goal: *that* is the goal of a lifetime" (as cited by Hillman, 1993, p. 235). The notion of goal is necessary for maintaining one's investment in the tremendous task of crafting a robust soul.

The patient always arrives with a goal in mind, a purposive fantasy for which he or she came to treatment, and without which there would be no patient and no therapist. This fantasy, in conjunction with the therapist's fantasy of treatment, is carried through the various operations along with the prima materia of the presenting problem. It is tortured, killed, dried, moistened, coagulated, and dissolved, always present in the room, penetrated and permeated by the shifting hand of Mercurius. As the psyche changes, so too does the goal.

Hillman (1993) described the goal as:

> tender, soft, like sugar, malleable as wax. This stone melts easily; it receives impression like a *tabula rasa* and then just as easily lets

> them go again. It asks to be affected, penetrated and, because transparent, seen through. As its borders are not fixed, its defense is yielding and its answers always indefinite. It allows itself to be pushed around without altering its substance. Like wax, its condition reacts to the climate of its surroundings. With the warmth of human touch, it takes the shape of the hands that hold it, remaining, nonetheless, self-consistent. . . . Any moment offers the fresh start, the innocence of a slate wiped clean.
>
> (p. 255)

With words like tender, soft, warmth, melt, wax, yielding, indefinite, react, and receive, one gets the *impression* that a well-worked psyche is far from the hardened hero idealized so often on screens across the nation. The psyche of rubedo is paradoxically always true to form and always receptive to new shape as it responds to that which is presented.

Moreover, the *rubitized* psyche has been awakened to a realization that the goal it had sought elsewhere, the archetypal pull of the hero's journey, has been obfuscating the fact that the goal has been and is still all around and fully disclosed. The reddening into life happens through the erotic pull of the world—the pleasure received through yielding to the beauty of the anima mundi. The redemption of the world to which the alchemist referred is not a transmutation of the world itself, but rather an awakening of one's senses to the glorious gem shinning in each thing—"an exaltation of the material body of the world" (Hillman, 1993, p. 265), an aesthetic awakening which pulls an individual out of subjective slumber into the world of things.

## References

Bachelard, G. (1987). *On poetic imagination and reverie*. Putnam, CT: Spring.

Berry, P. (1982). *Echo's subtle body: Contributions to an archetypal psychology*. Putnam, CT: Spring.

Bion, W. R. (1962). The psycho-analytic study of thinking. *International Journal of Psycho-Analysis*, *43*, 306–310. Retrieved from http://search.ebscohost.com/login.aspx?direct=true&db=pph&AN=IJP.043.0306A&site=ehost-live

Coppin, J. (1996). *Language in the Practice of Archetypal Psychotherapy* (Doctoral dissertation). Retrieved from ProQuest Digital Dissertations. (AAT 250069480)

Derrida, J. (1974). *Of grammatology* (G. C. Spivak, Trans.). Baltimore, MD: Johns Hopkins Press.

Drob, S. L. (2008). James Hillman on language: Escape from the linguistic prison. In S. Marlan (Ed.), *Archetypal psychologies: Reflections in honor of James Hillman* (pp. 153–168). New Orleans, LA: Spring Journal.

Freud, S. (1953). *The interpretation of dreams: The complete and definitive text* (J. Strachey & G. Zilboorg, Trans.). New York, NY: Basic Books. (Original work published 1900)

Freud, S. (1964). *New introductory lectures on psycho-analysis.* (W. J. H. Sprott, Trans.). New York, NY: W. W. Norton. (Original work published 1933)

Hillman, J. (1975). *Re-visioning psychology.* New York, NY: Harper and Row.

Hillman, J. (1980a). Silver and the white earth. *Spring*, *47*, 21–48.

Hillman, J. (1980b). The therapeutic value of alchemical language. In I. F. Baker (Ed.), *Methods of treatment in analytical psychology* (pp. 118–126). Fellvack: Bonz.

Hillman, J. (1981a). Alchemical blue and the unio mentalis. *Sulfur: A Literary Tri-quarterly of the Whole Art I*, 33–50.

Hillman, J. (1981b). Silver and the white earth (part two). *Spring*, *48*, 21–66.

Hillman, J. (1991). The yellowing of the work. In M. A. Mattoon (Ed.), *Personal and archetypal dynamics in the analytical relationship* (pp. 77–102). Einsiedeln, Switzerland: Daimon.

Hillman, J. (1993). Concerning the goal. *Sphinx*, *5*, 234–265.

Hillman, J. (1997). The seduction of black. *Spring*, *61*, 1–15.

Hillman, J. (2006). The azure vault: The caelum as experience. In L. Cowan (Ed.), *Edges of experience: Memory and emergence* (pp. 25–39). Einsiedeln, Switzerland: Daimon Verlag.

Jung, C. G. (1967). Symbols of transformation. In H. Read, M. Fordham, G. Adler, & W. McGuire (Eds.), *The collected works of C. G. Jung* (R. F. C. Hull, Trans.) (2nd ed., Vol. 5). Princeton, NJ: Princeton University Press. (Original work published 1912)

Jung, C. G. (1969). Concerning rebirth. In H. Read, M. Fordham, G. Adler, & W. McGuire (Eds.), *The collected works of C. G. Jung* (R. F. C. Hull, Trans.) (Vol. 9i, pp. 113–150). Princeton, NJ: Princeton University Press. (Original work published 1950)

Jung, C. G. (1970). Mysterium coniunctionis: An inquiry into the separation and synthesis of psychic opposites in alchemy. In H. Read, M. Fordham, G. Adler, & W. McGuire (Eds.), *The collected works of C. G. Jung* (R. F. C. Hull, Trans.) (2nd ed., Vol. 14). Princeton, NJ: Princeton University Press. (Original work published 1956)

Kugler, P. (1982). *The alchemy of discourse: Image, sound and psyche.* Einsiedeln, Switzerland: Daimon.

Lacan, J. (1981). *The language of the self: The function of language in psychoanalysis* (A. Wilden, Trans.). Baltimore, MD: Johns Hopkins Press. (Original work published 1953)

Lévi-Strauss, C. (1983). *Structural anthropology.* Chicago: University of Chicago Press. (Original work published 1958).

Lopez-Pedraza, R. (1977). *Hermes and his children.* Zurich, Switzerland: Spring.

Ovid. (1986). *Metamorphoses.* (A. D. Melville, Trans.). New York, NY: Oxford University Press.

Romanyshyn, R. (2002). *Ways of the heart: Essays toward an imaginal psychology.* Pittsburgh, PA: Trivium Publications.

Saussure, F. D. (2011). *Course in general linguistics.* (W. Baskin, Trans.). New York, NY: Columbia University Press. (Original work published 1916)

Schenk, R. (2006). The alchemical attitude of the analytic mind: An introductory

primer on prima material for initial beginners at the start. *Spring: A Journal of Archetype and Culture*, *74*, 151–173.
Thass-Thienemann, T. (1973). *The interpretation of language*. New York, NY: Jason Aronson.
Winnicott, D. W. (1971). *Playing and reality*. New York, NY: Basic Books.
Wittgenstein, L. (1953). *Philosophical investigations*. (G. E. M. Anscombe, Trans.). New York, NY: MacMillan.

Chapter 5

# Aesthetic sensibility

Hillman's two essays *The Anima Mundi: The Return to the Soul of the World* (1982) and *The Thought of the Heart* (1984) mark a significant change in the field of archetypal psychology. He has described this move as a shift in "the idea of depth from the psychology of the inner person to a psychology of things, a depth psychology of extraversion" (Hillman & Ventura, 1992, p. 53). Whereas his prior emphasis was clearly in favor of psychologizing and "reflection [that] takes place in terms other than those presented" (Hillman, 1975, p. 135), Hillman's more recent work has called for an aesthetic psychology, emphasizing "appearances as such, created as they are, in the forms with which they are given, sense data, bare facts, Venus Nudata" (Hillman, 1992, p. 43).[1]

Hillman (1992) has situated the psychology of aesthetics in the temple of Aphrodite, stating: "She appears above all in the *manifest*, not as content of it (for that remains available only to understanding), but as the manifest visible image, the displayed presentation" (p. 56). Whereas critics like Tacey (1998) have called this a "disastrous outbreak of overt contradiction" (p. 230), perhaps this move is an explication of the polytheistic psychology Hillman has claimed to represent, a shift in focus from a psychology of the invisible (Hades) to a psychology of presentation (Aphrodite).

With his exposition on beauty, Hillman has continued his love of image, but has brought that love from an intrapsychic notion of *anima* to a transpsychic notion of *anima mundi*—an idea deriving out of the platonic and neoplatonic philosophical traditions. Hillman (1992) wrote " 'Taking in' means interiorizing the object into itself, into its image so that *its* imagination is activated (rather than ours)" (p. 48), a kind of reverie that attempts to see the world through the eyes of another creature. The painter Franz Marc expressed a similar argument: "it is a poverty-stricken convention to place animals into landscapes as seen by men; instead we should contemplate the soul of the animal to divine its way of sight" (as cited in Bleakley, 1995, p. 391).

This kind of imagination requires a quickening of the animal nature of the heart, what Hillman (1992) has referred to as the heart "awakened into life by a roar" (p. 64)—an aesthetic response that cuts through the anesthetized slumber of the contemporary individual and draws his or her attention to the beauty of the particular.

An aesthetic psychotherapy presents a strong counterforce to the mechanized and manualized forms of treatment—the very negation of particularity and sensual response. Bleakley (1995) has offered an alternative to such senseless systems, arguing for "an aesthetic of information" (p. 387) akin to the highly attuned attention of the hunter tracking an animal. The psychotherapist opens his or her senses to the patient's form, noting a footprint here, a scent there, and piecing the sensual data together with intuition, cognition, and imagination. These impressions are then offered back to the patient, thereby providing an opportunity for internalizing, or awakening to, his or her own aesthetic sensibility.

Managed care and the desire for a quick fix have led to a surge of treatment styles that strictly target function, that is, behavior. Whereas such treatments have demonstrated success empirically, it could be argued that treating function with little to no attention to form, that is, the aesthetics of the therapeutic relationship and the patient's life, results in collusion with a culture-wide negation of the human as animal. Following the German zoologist Adolf Portmann's (1986) argument that an animal's presentational display is in the service of beauty, Bleakley (1995) has noted the very same need to be seen and to see aesthetically as a primary feature of the human animal. Moreover, it could be argued that the atrophy of one's aesthetic sense could very well be at the root of many functional disorders.

Several archetypal psychologists, such as Berry (1984), Schenk (1989), Hillman (1992), Bleakley (1995) and Romanyshyn (2002), have pointed towards an alternative approach that offers a radical reorientation, placing aesthetics as primary, as both medium and goal (Bleakley, 1995). Aesthetic psychotherapy places "noticing prior to interpretation" (p. 390) differentiation of presentation prior to elimination of pathology, and extends the concern of psychotherapy from the function of the subject to the way in which the patient is responding to the things of the world, people, and his or her own being.

Aesthetic sensibility, the response of the heart to the presentation of things, is a requirement of soul; "psyche is the life of our aesthetic responses" (Hillman, 1992, p. 39). The soul feeds on beauty. However, this notion of beauty is not to be mistaken for the flowery soft beauty typically associated to this term. Rather, as Plotinus stated: "We possess beauty when we are true to our own being; ugliness is in going over to another order" (as cited in Hillman, 1992, p. 59). Analogous to the animal's evaluation through scent, this mode of responding to the beautiful undercuts detached cognition with a response rooted in immediacy and a corresponding remembrance of the cosmology to which one belongs.

The Greek notion of *Kosmos* is an idea rooted in aesthetics: "it referred to the right placing of the multiple things of the world, their ordered arrangement" (Hillman, 1992, p. 44). A cosmological perspective upholds the singular and unique, whereas the notion of universe blends things together into a unified whole. When the particular is lost in place of the general, one loses the essential connection to beauty, and beauty is nothing less than the way "the Gods touch our senses, reach the heart, and attract us into life" (p. 45). Jung's (1929/1968) statement "the gods have become diseases" (p. 113) has shown its veracity in relation to both the individual's pathology as well as the sickness of the world soul. When the Gods no longer capture our attention through beauty, they are relegated to expression through symptom, demonstrating the ways in which we have moved into another order.

Bleakley (1995) noted "an animalizing eye and an animalizing aesthetic may be educated through attention to metaphors of form as well as actual form, although these metaphors appear to have greater vitality if they stay close to the biological" (p. 390). Staying close to the biological requires a specific education—an experiential education based in a sharpening of perception. To put it bluntly, the development of an aesthetic sensibility requires the individual to go outside and pay attention, stepping both feet into the poetics of place.

The animal metaphors we use in daily vernacular are not arbitrary. They display in a very simple way what Hillman means by the soul of the world. Every thing has soul, that is, an expression of meaning, and speaks soul through presentation. The movements, sounds, colors, shapes, textures, behaviors of the natural world all tell a story, and the skill of hearing these stories is the ground from which an aesthetic sensibility is formed.

Appreciation of the *anima mundi* gives way to a profound expansion of an individual's circle of relatedness. Hillman (1992) noted "intimacy occurs when we live in a world of particular, concrete events, noticeable for what [William] James called their 'eachness' " (p. 120). The *res extensa* of Descartes, a dead world of exploitable objects, is revived for any individual who lives from the notion that nature, as Alfred North Whitehead (1938/1968) claimed, is alive, constantly revealing itself through the particularity of its presentation.

Psychotherapy, in its adherence to the subjective and inter-subjective domains, places undue responsibility on the shoulders of the individual and the family. Hillman (1992) has admonished psychotherapists to differentiate between "the neurosis of self and neurosis of world, psychopathology of self and psychopathology of world" (p. 93). At the center of this "anesthetized slumber of subjectivism" (p. 100) is a loss of responsivity to those things that fall outside one's subjective domain. The psychotherapist has an ethical obligation to help awaken the patient's animal sensibility and initiate the individual's return to their place "in the family of things" (Oliver, 1993, p. 110).

Social psychological research investigating collective constructionist theory has demonstrated that construction of the self and the way in which individuals build self-esteem is in direct relation to the idiosyncratic perspectives and methods sanctioned by the culture to which he or she belongs (Kitayama, Matsumoto, Markus, & Norasakkunkit, 1997). Despite evidence suggesting that important attributes of the self are socially constructed, the trend in psychotherapy is to center attention on the personal factors relating to the etiology and prognosis of the psychological disorder. Hillman (2006) has argued that the move of turning inward, so ubiquitous in therapy, is in actuality emblematic of the same narcissistic tendency that therapy sets out to treat. He has pointed to Freud's description of narcissism as an inversion of object libido away from the world, toward the individual ego, and suggested that further introversion ignores the fact that for the narcissistic individual the call of beauty, the spell of the sensuous (Abram, 1996), has become repressed, no longer pulling the individual into the world through aesthetic appreciation.

Much of the responsibility is placed on the parents of the individual, particularly the mother's inadequate mirroring (Kohut, 1971), leaving the impact of the declining quality of schools, overworked teachers, reduced funding for public programs, overly processed high calorie foods, and oppressive architecture as unexamined contributing factors. Without analysis of the social unconscious, the individual is forced to bare the burden of socially constructed pathology, and energy that could be directed towards social change is inverted and used to become a more sensitive introverted individual (Hillman & Ventura, 1992).

Encouraging patients to develop better coping skills reinforces conformity to a neurotic world. More effective adaptation is a misdirection of the problem; the symptom is bound to shift, thus creating another problem to which one must adapt. Alternatively, Hillman (1992) has argued for an expansion of etiological concern to include "the repressed unconsciousness projecting from the world of things" (p. 100).

Juan Tubert-Oklander (2006) has argued that the unconscious phenomena that psychoanalysis aims at making conscious are not simply isolated idiosyncratic features of the individual's mind, but rather, as social psychological research has indicated, "the inter- and transpersonal processes pervade the individual, thus determining his or her experience and behavior, and becoming the deepest stratum of the unconscious" (p. 146). The pervading split between so-called interior and exterior is an antiquated notion discredited by a variety of fields ranging from neuroscience, to physics, to developmental psychology. Every intrapsychic phenomenon is culturally-historically situated (Cushman, 1996). In addition, Tubert-Oklander has argued that the psychoanalytic tendency to exclusively focus attention on the intrapsychic elements of the patient's presenting material may be an act of denial effectively obscuring pathogenic features of society and further strengthening dominant systems of authority.

Watkins and Shulman (2008) have suggested that the depth psychological sensibility of listening to and following the dynamic vicissitudes of the symptom must not only lead the therapist and patient into analysis of the individual soul and its wounds, but also the soul and wounds of the community. They offer a triple orientation: "toward the symptom, toward the listener's theoretical and ideological commitments, and toward surrounding social and institutional contexts" (p. 54).

The various schools of psychoanalysis are fundamentally subversive in their attempt at uncovering the hidden and repressed and affording value to that which has been forgotten; however, as analysis has become relegated to strict focus on the inter and intrasubjective, its subversive potency has diminished, and as Hillman and Ventura (1992) noted, "people are getting more and more sensitive, and the world is getting worse and worse" (p. 3).

An aesthetic sensibility invites the psychotherapist and patient to stand side by side and turn towards the world, slowing down, and widening the sphere of importance beyond the intrapsychic, developmental, and family system. In taking time to notice the individual's aesthetic response to political, environmental, and communal happenings, events begin to take on new significance, and soul is once again afforded its proper place in the world of things.

## Note

1 Whereas Hillman's turn to the world contains within it a strong but implicit reliance on key concepts from phenomenology, a review of the interrelations between archetypal psychology and phenomenology is beyond the scope of this study. The reader is referred to Michael Sipiora's (1999) essay entitled "The Anima Mundi and the Fourfold: Hillman and Heidegger on the 'Idea' of the World."

## References

Abram, D. (1996). *The spell of the sensuous: Perception and language in a more-than-human world*. New York, NY: Random House.

Berry, P. (1984). Jung's early psychiatric writing: The emergence of a psychopoetics (Unpublished Doctoral Dissertation). University of Dallas, Dallas, TX.

Bleakley, A. (1995). Animalizing and shamanizing: Animal presence in shamanism and archetypal psychology (Unpublished Doctoral Dissertation). University of Sussex, East Sussex, UK.

Cushman, P. (1996). *Constructing the self, constructing America: A cultural history of psychotherapy*. New York, NY: Addison-Wesley.

Hillman, J. (1975). *Re-visioning psychology*. New York, NY: Harper and Row.

Hillman, J. (1982). *Anima mundi: The return of the soul of the world*. Dallas, TX: Spring.

Hillman, J. (1984). *The thought of the heart*. Dallas, TX: Spring.

Hillman, J. (1992). *The thought of the heart and the soul of the world*. Putnam, CT: Spring Publications, Inc.

Hillman, J., & Ventura, M. (1992). *We've had a hundred years of psychotherapy—and the world's getting worse*. New York, NY: HarperOne.

Hillman, J. (2006). *City and soul*. Putnam, CT: Spring.

Jung, C. G. (1968). Commentary on the secret of the golden flower. In H. Read, M. Fordham, G. Adler, & W. McGuire (Eds.), *The collected works of C. G. Jung* (R. F. C. Hull, Trans.) (Vol. 13, pp. 1–56). Princeton, NJ: Princeton University Press. (Original work published 1929)

Kitayama, S., Matsumoto, H., Markus, H. R., & Norasakkunkit, V. (1997). Individual and collective processes in the construction of the self: Self-enhancement in the United States and self-criticism in Japan. *Journal of Personality and Social Psychology*, 72(6), 1245–1266.

Kohut, H. (1971). *The analysis of the self: A systematic approach to the psychoanalytic treatment of narcissistic personality disorders*. Chicago: University of Chicago Press.

Oliver, M. (1993). *New and selected poems*. Boston, CT: Beacon Press.

Portmann, A. (1986). The orientation and world-relation of animals. *Spring*, *53*, 1–15.

Romanyshyn, R. (2002). *Ways of the heart: Essays toward an imaginal psychology*. Pittsburgh, PA: Trivium Publications.

Schenk, R. (1989). The soul of beauty: A psychological investigation of appearance (Unpublished Doctoral Dissertation). University of Dallas, Dallas, TX.

Tacey, D. (1998). Twisting and turning with James Hillman: From anima to world soul, from academia to pop. In A. Casement (Ed.) *Post-Jungians today: Key papers in contemporary analytical psychology*. New York, NY: Routledge.

Tubert-Oklander, J. (2006). The individual, the group and society: Their psychoanalytic inquiry. *International Forum of Psychoanalysis*, *15*, 146–150.

Watkins, M., & Shulman, H. (2008). *Toward psychologies of liberation*. New York, NY: Palgrave Macmillan.

Whitehead, A. N. (1968). *Modes of thought*. New York: Simon and Schuster. (Original work published 1938).

Chapter 6

# Reflections and undoing

## Reflections

Throughout this study, I have attempted to gather the primary ingredients for an archetypal psychotherapy—a method of construction in response to Hillman's deconstruction, a Hephaestian fantasy of collecting bits of method, weaving them together with dreams, fantasy images, and clinical vignettes in an effort to craft a depiction of the particular style taken up by archetypal psychotherapy.

The face of archetypal psychotherapy that has taken form is one in which the phenomenal presentation of psychic image is given radical autonomy and privilege. As an imaginal psychology, archetypal psychotherapy is concerned with preservation of the complexity and multiple meanings of the image, careful attention to the presentation of the image through differentiating its particular features and clarifying its context, mood, and scene, and the use of language that vivifies the poetic basis of mind—uncovering the images hidden in words, feelings, and events. Interpretations, when made, are expressed with a sense of their own relativity—that each thing known carries with it another side. Singleness of meaning is supplanted by a multitude of analogical relationships linking image and waking life, an ever-shifting cascade of significance. Ego development is supplanted by the cultivation of an imaginal ego—relativized by the many centers of the psyche, a willingness to die many deaths. Reality testing is supplanted by the development of an image-sense—an aesthetic sensibility skilled in the craft of imaginal description, taking up a style mimetic to the particular presentation. Personal associations, amplifications, and interpretations are positioned as secondary to aesthetic encounters with imagination.

The barrage of information one receives when working as a therapist requires an organizing structure. Theorists and practitioners are classed based on where they locate their organizing principle. An archetypal approach strives for the widest possible field of inclusion: behaviors, thoughts, defenses, emotions, transference derivatives, symbols—all are imagined as images, expressions of a psyche that is always located in one archetypal fantasy or another. Locating this location, through a qualitatively differentiated tradition like classical mythology, alchemy, or astrology offers the wide range of individual experience a home within the structures of collective experience, imbues the experience with profound value, excites the imagination of both therapist and patient, and helps the individual recognize his or her place as an integral member in a Kosmos of depth and meaning.

## Undoing

From the outset, this work was destined to fail. Archetypal psychotherapy is styled in multiples, polytheism, and description through negation. The efforts I have made towards construction must be, at the end, deconstructed. To affirm that these pages contain *the* style of archetypal psychotherapy would be utterly false, a codification of a tradition that, to be true to itself, must remain mercurial and polycentric, *many centered.*

This work has offered a partial depiction of one center among many, a momentary snap shot of an always-shifting image. My aim in providing this image is to inspire further imaging, not to settle the matter, but to open it up, not to conclude but to begin.

# Index